HOW SOCIETY INFLUENCES ORGANIZATIONAL RESOURCE CHANGES

JOHN LOK

Copyright

Contents

Preface

Introduction

Any organizations must need resources to be provided in order to suppky for their organizational development. However, resouces may include human resources, equipment facilities resources , earth natural resource e.g. land, water wood, gas et. building material resources, even working time resources , technological etc. different kinds of resources. Thus, it seems that any organizations must need some resources to help their organizational daily operation in success. The question concerns what the best resources used strategies to be achieve the most efficiency or the best performance to be organizational development. How can business apply right or reasonable science management principle to manage that businesses effectively and efficiently in order to achieve sale and profit raising aim in the least resource suitation? Otherwise, applying wrong or unreasonable science management principle , it can bring what disadvantages or negative impacts to the businesses. IN my this chapter, I shall attempt to indicate above questions . Readers can have more clear view whether why the kinds of science resource management methods are not suitable to be applied to the kind of organizations to bring negative impact consequences.

How social change influences human behavioral change ? Why human behavior may be influenced by social change? Our individual behavior whether can be influenced to bring negative or positive attitude by social change? I shall attempt to indicate cases to explain whether our individual behavior can be influenced to changed by social environment change. Readers can have more understand how and why social change may influence our behavior in possible. Behavioral economy is one useful and fun social subject. Behavioral economists ususally research how and why human behaviors may influence economy growth or recession, or how and why economy environment changing factor may influence human behavior changes.

Prologue

Tablof content

Chapter 1 How social change influences organizational ecommerce development

● Why internet may be main technology resource to organizations? p.3-11

● Why doe e-commerce organization believe (e-webstore design, e-leaders and e-managers) will be main organizational resources?

Chapter 2 How social change influences organizational resource useful strategy

● HR resource p.12-25

● Time resource

   Organization efficient using resources economic method

● What is efficient use of resources to any organizations in economics?

● What is meant by economic using of resource to organizations?
p. 26-42

   The relationship between organization resources using and social resources

● Social resource means p.43-60

● Can responding to resource scarcity help some kinds business grow?

   Chapter 3

Amazon ecommerce organization resource useful strategy

● How management accounting cocept can help Amazon

publish to manage its cost effectively in order to increase its profit or e-books or paper books sale ability. p.61-75

● How mental (managerial) accounting concept helps Amazon publish to make investment decision?

● Can robots perform management accounting analysis tasks

● Why does organizational resource budget need?

● How can the laptop computer seller applies management accounting data to analyze whether which is the main factor to influence laptop buyer behavior changes?

Chapter 4 How social change influence market resource supply

The relationship between resource shortage and consumer behavior

Can resource shortage influence consumer behavior changes? p.76-85

Can bring either positive or negative or both impact to change consumer behavior when the consumer begins to feel resource shrtage occurrence to choose to buy the kind of product or consume the kind of service?

How does a consumer make choice with scarce resources?

Do they have relationship between organizational technology resource economic behavior and social needs?

Why have they interaction to influence resource supply between orgaizations and societies?

How social change influences organizational ecommerce rategy

Why does in this e-commerce organization situation, online webstore speed must be the most important factor to influence its sale success. Information technology internet speed, online webstore design, online transation convenience transaction feeling (tangibale and intangible

The relationship between social change and human behavior

How human productive behavior may influence economic development p.128-135

● New Zealand farmer individual wine productive behavior

● America high technological productive behavior

● China share market investing behavior

I

How social change influences organizational ecommerce development

New economy brings new way of resource management. The old loyalty and job security -based organization changes, organizations know that the assets are largely made up employees (HRM), but many new organizations begin to believe technology is important assets, such as Amazon is global ecommerce delivery service organization. It seems internet high technology is its important intangible resource to help it earn global e-buyers number increases . So , many organizations began to believe that technology will be important resource, such as internet can provide online business chance. With all the businesses are taking full advantage of internet, for example, the US department estimates that the value of retail e-commerce in 2000 year was about $25 billion, which represents less than 1% of US retail sales. Despite this, interest in e-business remains high.

● Why internet may be main technology resource to organizations?

E-commere needs strategy in order to win competitors, questions include: What criteria do customers use to choose between our firms and competitors? How do the best employees decision whether to join? What business environment attracts and keeps the best suppliers making with our firms? What characteristics draw the most royal invesdtors to our firms? e.g. Amazon . com's web site and Wal-mart's can apply internet technology resource to create each e-store to let e-buyers to choose any kinds of products to buy athome conveniently. Hence, internet technology, even future other kinds of new technology may be main technology resources to organizations, when they can help organizations to raise sale competitive effort.

I mean that digital economy will be one kind new digital resource to future any organizations. The essential piece is the knowledge, it is what give it life and what makes it an interesting and fulifulling purchase and sale channel for people to spend their time , such as e-commerce virtual organization may be leaded to let purchase and ale transactions carry on easily from online websites. Hence, internet may be main knowledge management (intellectual capital) resource to any e-commerce organizations. It is about the storage, transfer knowledge.

For Amazon publish example, e-books will be knowledge as

an object, like a book in library. Amazon can apply internet technology to help it to sell any author's ebooks from its book estores. So, ebooks are Amazon's knowledge resources to help it to create readers incomes. E-books is intangible knowledge resource to Amazon . Any authors' paper and ebooks will be sold cheap price to help Amazon to attract global readers to choose to buy its ebooks from its different countries e-webstores at home conveniently.

Hence, any e-commerce organizations also need HRM (emanagers) to help them to deliver a superior value (world class capabilities) in both te virtual and physical world. E-management will be another main human resources to e-commerce organizations. Why does e-management will be future main HRM resource to e-commerce organization? The reasons may include:

E-management demands in sort of managerial/e-commerce sale strategy effort, skills at positioning the firm within a networm of industries, e-management also demands the ability to see how the firm fits into a value creation-e-management is different because doing it work requires the e-engineering of business eco-systems, e-management demands the ability to be connected to thousands of inputs about specific changes among many industry participants , such as suppliers , customers, employees, competitors, media and shareholders.

Effective e-management requires the ability to monitor developments that can change with unusually high frequency. However, it is also essential that e-managers distinguish between the few meaningful inputs and the many inputs that have limited significance, ability to sustain organizational change, effectie e-managers monitor changes in their markets. So, instead of e-commerce organizations need to employ talent e-managment staffs to help them to manage overall e-commerce organizations. E-leading staffs (HRM) is another main HRM need. E-leaders need to know how to design online brochures, e.g. online brochures simply involved putting a company's market materials on the web. in order to attract or persuade online buyers visit its websites and choose the most right price of product to buy easily. E-leaders need to lead front-office transactions which involved putting customer facing customers , such as placing on order on the web when leaving back-office activities, such as order fulfillment unchanged.

E-leaders also need to integrate online online purchase transactions in which a firm actually linked its front -office and back -office systems and processes in a fashion, e.g. most companies have developed online brochures , in order to let online advertisement tool to attract e-buyer individual purchase choice from its webstores. Hence, future any e-commerce organizations must need (HRM (e-leaders and e-managers) to help them to bring innovation in order to achieve maximize profit aim. So, internet webstores, e-leaders , e-managers may be future e-commerce organization main resources. So, e-commerce organizations, manages are actors at three levels: In the front line , as entrepreneurs, in the middle , as facilitators, and integrators, at the top as institution builders.

Hence, future new economical society, it creates e-commerce organizations number increases, when consumers began to accept online purchase transaction activities. Hence, it causes e-commerce began to feel internet (e-webstores, e-leaders, e-managers), they will be the most influential resources (intangible knowledge managment and tangible URM both resourcees to influence their success or failure.

● Why doe e-commerce organization believe (e-webstore design, e-leaders and e-managers) will be main organizational resources?

The most important question: It asks when e-buyers visit their webstores, wo are their target customers and shich needs of theirs are their trying to satisfy? For exap,e many airlines , e.g. American airlines, China airlines began to feel online e-tickets sale channel is more easily than paper ticket shop sale channel, because many air passengers began to accept e-ticket/online ticket purchase choice more than visiting airline shops . They feel that they do not want to waste time to visit airline shops. They like to pre-book to buy e-ticket to pay from the airline e-websote conveniently. Hence, e-webstore design knowledge management , e-leaders and e-management webstore management skill will be future any one e-commerce organizations their main tangible and intangible resources (assets) to help their e-commerce businesses development.

On conclusion, I believe that the current economy is not a high-tech economy or an internet economy, not an m-commerce economy , but instead customer econoomy. Customers need to gather with information and access, they are demanding, fair, global price, they are demanding that compares deal with them using the distribution channel , they choose manufacturing direct and through dealers and retailers. Base on those factors, they encourage future many e-commerce organizations cause organization change traditional resouce concept, such as land, capital equipment, tangible resource began to change to e-commerce organization's intangibel and tangible resource, such as knowledge management to e-online web store design skills, e-leaders and e-managers e-stores sale management strategy and e-buyer product research and brochure online advertisement design skill. All of these knowledge management skill will be future organizations' main resources to help them to create new economic competition effort.

Organization resources defination

What are organizational resources ? What do organizational resources mean? What kinds of organizational resources are needed? What negative impact may be influenced if organizations lack enough resources to influence organizational development? Does working time belong to organizational time resources to influence employee individual efficiency e.g. how arranging enough employee to do the identified task in the most short time in order to achieve the most efficient performane? I shall attempt to identify examples to explain above questions as below:

In general, organizational resources are all assets, that are available to a firm for use during the production process. The four basic types of organizational resources are human, monetary , raw materials and capital. Organizational resources are combined, used and transofrmed to finished products during the production process. For organizational human resource example, human resource activities full under the following five core functions: staffing, development, compensation, safety and health core functions.

● HR resource

HR conducts a wide variety of activities. However, in any organizations, the major resources used by organizations are often described as follow (1) human resources (2) financial respirces (3) physical resources and (4) information resources. Managers are responsible for acquring and managing the resources to accomplosh goals. Hence, in organizational HR aspect, it may include these function, such as retirement and selection, performance management , learning and development, succession planning, compensation and benefits, human resource information systems. Because considering that for many organizations employees themselves represent a significant cost to the business, if the organization can use its employees in efficiency.

Then, it can avoid human resource in excess or in surplus on wasting challenge. Then , its employee cost or salary can be reduced. I t means that it does not need to employ in excess employees number, but the organization can still achieve itself the most efficient performance. Hence, any organizations must need to learn how to avoid " in excess employees number supply or wasting employee working behaviors" challenge . Because if some tasks do not need many employees to work together, it can still be achieved efficiency . Then , the organization ought not employee too many or excess employees to finish the kind of task. Thus, learning how to use efficient human resources, it can help organizations to avoid wasting working time to any departments employees. For example, when one factory has limited land to be supplied to become warehouse in order to help it to keep sticks. If it has excess logistic or factory workers number. Then, they are wasting working time to do not important tasks in warehouse, it means that if the factory has only one warehouse, but its area is small, it can allow maximum 50 workers to stay in the warehouse , but the warehouse has above 100 workers are staying to deliver goods in the small warehouse . Then, they must not actieve the most efficiency , even their delivery or transport goods performance will be influenced to worse by noise and crowd warehouse working environment. Hence, excess employees number in any working environment, which can not improve organizational performance or riase efficiency any organizations can not neglect " excess employees number" organizatinal HR resource arranging issue.

The solution concerns arranging the most right or the most exact empllyees number in order to supply to any organizational departments. Then, the organization can avoid wasting employee individual talent, reducing employing cost, improvig performance, achieving the most efficiency. Resource capacity means resource pool who are available in the organization to take up to appropriate human resource arrangement to assist any departmental development in long term efficiency. Hence, organizational human rsources may become talent tangible assets or foolish tangible assets. It depends on how the organization's resource capacity tasks arrangement to every employee in different departments. If the organization neglects how to arrange every employee task in the most exact or the most appropriate employees number in the department.

The department's efficiency must be caused worse, because excess employees number, it can not help it to achieve the most efficiency aim, even it may influence the excess employees , themselves feel waste working hours to do the not essential or not important tasks. Then, the organization may cause talent employee to become foolish employee. Otherwise, the organization's efficiency to be worse, because when the department has not enough employees to work. Then , any one employee may feel hard to work, his/her emotion may be influenced to negative, then his/

her workig behavior may b inefficiency or lazy working. On consequence, the organization may bring economic loss, due to employee individual lasy working behavior, negative working emotion, even high working pressure may be caused, when one employee needs to do more , then the employee's task, but his/her salary can not increase. He/she will feel unfair to compare the another department employee, he /she does not need to spend long working hours or overtime to work per day. SO, any organization needs to avoid shortage employee supply or excess employee supply issue to any departments. Appropriare employees number is the best strategy in order to raise overall organizational efficiency.

● Time resource

Instead of human resource, land, raw material, earth natural resource, electricity, gas may be organization resources . Whether time may be organizational resources, organizational time management vires time as a scarce resource that must be invested as effectivity. Time is an infinite resource . If not properly managed on in an organization. It can have a negative impact on both employer's and employee's productivity. So, organizations should ensure that workers are well equipped to manage time in their duties.So, in management view, any organization managers must need to consider how to manage time, eg . how to arrange employees to work in different departments in order to achieve the most efficiency. They need to understand which resources are in short supply and focus on the prioritizing work across shared resources, they need agree on a common approach, they also need to realize resource management is an ongoing process. Thus, time is an often ignored but invaluable resource in any organization. All activities be it procurement.

An organization's time, in contrast, goes largely unmanaged. Although, phone calls, email, instant messages , meetings, they are general daily tasks to any organizations managers, but mangers need to know how to arrange the most urgent tasks in prior. For example, if the manager can not arrange a meeting to the discuss client tomorroe, as well as the manager needs to spend two hours to meeting with overall 200 employees to discuss how to solve improving efficiency challenge tomorroe. So, this manager needs to make choice whether he ought spend two hours meeting to the business client, or two hours meeting to 200 employees. If he chooses to meet the business client tomorrow, he will help his firm to win the important business chance, but he can not discuss how to improve efficiency in order to find the best method to let 200 employees to know tomorrow. Thus, tomorrow time management will be one importat time resource to the manager. The manager needs to arrange tomorrow two hours time how to plan business meting or efficiency imporvement meerting either to his 200 employees or the one business client. Because if the manager decided to meet the client, he must need to spend today time to aplan or organize how to arrange either business proposal content for the business client or organizational operational challenge questions and solutions for his 200 employees . So, today time management is also important time resource to influence tomorrow either the success business meeting or the organizational 200 employees meeting. So, it seems that time management may be one important resource to any managers more than general employees in any organizations.

If the manager can know how to manager his/her time to

do any prior tasks, then he/she may help the organization to raise efficiency or improve performance. Otherwise, if the manager can not know how arrange what prior urgent task needs to be finished. Then, worse performance or inefficiency may be influenced to cause. So, if the organization manager can know how to make time arrangement, I believe that he can help the organization employees to raise efficiency more easily.

Organization efficient using resources economic method
In behavioral economic view , any organizations can attempt to apply behavioral economy method to use resources efficiently. Organizational excellence framework performance measurement takes a systematic approach . One of the most effective ways of using resources and minimizing that use of work. Calculating task cost in the most efficient economic method to help organizations to reduce cost and avoid resources waste, e.g. using resource management software, technology, planning and taking a systematic approach , which aims to manage the most efficient steps to follow to finish or implement each task in the most shor time as well as avoiding excess employees number.
Organizational resource efficiency means using the organization's limited resources in a sustainable manner when minimising impacts on the organization performance. It allows the organization to create more with less and to deliver greater value with less money. HR, raw material, technology input to carry on any organizational resources efficiently ? Management is the process of using organizational resources to achieve organizational goals of using organizational resources to achieve organizational goals effectively and efficiently through planning ,

organizing , leading and controlling. An efficient organization makes the most productive use of its resource in the most short time and the most eficiency and the least cost aspects.

● What is efficient use of resources to any organizations in economics?

Economic efficiency implies an economic state in which every resource is optimially allocated to serve each individual or entity in the best way when minimizing waste and inefficiency. whan an economy is economically efficient, any changes made to assist one entity would harm another . Hence, budget how much spending on resources, e.g. employee saley, office and/or plant technological equipment facilities , before making resource expenditure spending decision. Budget is essnetial to help the organization to deduce resource using and excess purchase waste since budget and resource of organizations have interlock or interconnet relationship. If the organization can make exact udget, then it can avoid excess expenditure or waste resource to use. So, organizations need to acquire a talented resource pool , that can lead projects to success, when any kinds of resources are achieved to be supplied to use inn enough . For example, using an effective enterprise resource management system that delivers capabilities. Regardless of the approach and tools used, organizations must determine how to balance to use any kinds of resources efficiently. Thus, in organizational efficient resource using behavioral economy view, the organizational efficiency factor means that influences the efficiency of the organization's use if its resources can be both internal and external, e.g. how implementing strategic plans, they may include selecting what methods and resources to use, and leadning employees on guideline, working in coalitions with organizations around to deliver those needs in the most resource efficient way.

In organizational studies, resource managemetn is the efficient and one resource management technique of resource leveling, of finding the answers to the question, how to use available resource efficiently, effectively and economically ot organization resource expense. SO , resource management is the process of allocating resources and allocating.

● What is meant by economic using of resource to organizations?

Economic resources are the factors used in producing goods or providing services. Economic resources can be divied into human resources, such as labors and management, and non humann resource, such as land, capital , goods, finished resources and technology , for example, natural resource is a key input in the production process that stimulates economic growth. Natural resources have limited direct economic use in satisfying human need, but transforming them into goods and services enhances their economic value to the socirty. So, if the country has many organizations know how to use their natural resources input in that production processes. Then, they can create themselves economic benefits directly and attribute economic benefit to society indirectly.

Thus, the types of economic organizations can be identified, there are subsistence recipreocal exchange with subsistence, peasant with primary reliance on self-produced food, but containing some exhange elements, market-commercial , redistribution or state socialist. Thus organizations need to learn hoe to use themselves organizational resources efficiently. Organizational resources are all assets that are to a firm for use during the production process. The four basic types of organizational resources are human, monetary, raw material and capital. Organizational resources are combined , used and transformed into finished products during the production process. So, a business that understands how to use resources efficiently. resource management is the process of allocating resources in order for a company to grow easily.

Organizational economic is used to study transactions within individual firms and determine management approach to managing resources. It is broken down into thee major subjects: agency theory, transaction cost economic and property rights theory. Agency theory is a priinciple that is used to explain and resolve issues in the relationship between business principles and their agents. Most commonly, that relationship is the one between shareholders as principles, and company executives as agents. Agency theory is used to understand the relationship between agents and principals. The agent represents the principal in a particular business transaction and is expected to represent the best interests of the principal without regard for seld interest. So, when the relationship between shreholders and company executives is kept the best.

Transaction cost economic is understood as alternative modes of organizing transactions (governance structure, such as markets, firms and bureaus) that mininize transactions costs. This, cost is the primary determinant of such as firm's decision whether it is the most right (the best) or the worst decision. It will influence the firm ho to spend resource behavior. The cost other than the money price that are incurred in trading good and service. SO, if the organization can often make the best decision to carry on any activites. It will avoid to waste resources efficiently. For example, if transaction cost influces the commission, paid to a stockbroker for completing a share deal and booking fee charges when purchase concert tickets. The cost of travel and time to complete an exhange , it means that transaction cost. So if the organization can make the best or the most reasonable decision to carry on any business activities. Then, its transaction cost can be influenced to reduce the most level in order to bring resources economic benefit. e.g. sunk costs are indpeendent of any event and should not resulting from economic trade in a market.

Property right theory means contracted choice, through ownership, property rights theour clarifies the firm's boundary choice. The maon egal property rights are the right of possession, the righ tof excession. So, for the efficiency of property rights al scarce resources are owned by someone. IN the right property rights approsed to the theory of the firm, I assume that in the case of sale ownership by party-property rights define the theoretical and legal ownership of resources and how resources can be used by organizatin. So, above three major organizational theories can assist organizations to know how to spend resources efficiently.

II

How social change influences organizational resource useful strategy

New economy brings new way of resource management. The old loyalty and job security -based organization changes, organizations know that the assets are largely made up employees (HRM), but many new organizations begin to believe technology is important assets, such as Amazon is global ecommerce delivery service organization. It seems internet high technology is its important intangible resource to help it earn global e-buyers number increases . So , many organizations began to believe that technology will be important resource, such as internet can provide online business chance. With all the businesses are taking full advantage of internet, for example, the US department estimates that the value of retail e-commerce in 2000 year was about $25 billion, which represents less than 1% of US retail sales. Despite this, interest in e-business remains high.

● Why internet may be main technology resource to organizations?

E-commere needs strategy in order to win competitors, questions include: What criteria do customers use to choose between our firms and competitors? How do the best employees decision whether to join? What business environment attracts and keeps the best suppliers making with our firms? What characteristics draw the most royal invesdtors to our firms? e.g. Amazon . com's web site and Wal-mart's can apply internet technology resource to create each e-store to let e-buyers to choose any kinds of products to buy athome conveniently. Hence, internet technology, even future other kinds of new technology may be main technology resources to organizations, when they can help organizations to raise sale competitive effort.

I mean that digital economy will be one kind new digital resource to future any organizations. The essential piece is the knowledge, it is what give it life and what makes it an interesting and fulifulling purchase and sale channel for people to spend their time , such as e-commerce virtual organization may be leaded to let purchase and ale transactions carry on easily from online websites. Hence, internet may be main knowledge management (intellectual capital) resource to any e-commerce organizations. It is about the storage, transfer knowledge.

For Amazon publish example, e-books will be knowledge as

an object, like a book in library. Amazon can apply internet technology to help it to sell any author's ebooks from its book estores. So, ebooks are Amazon's knowledge resources to help it to create readers incomes. E-books is intangible knowledge resource to Amazon . Any authors' paper and ebooks will be sold cheap price to help Amazon to attract global readers to choose to buy its ebooks from its different countries e-webstores at home conveniently.

Hence, any e-commerce organizations also need HRM (emanagers) to help them to deliver a superior value (world class capabilities) in both te virtual and physical world. E-management will be another main human resources to e-commerce organizations. Why does e-management will be future main HRM resource to e-commerce organization? The reasons may include:

E-management demands in sort of managerial/e-commerce sale strategy effort, skills at positioning the firm within a networm of industries, e-management also demands the ability to see how the firm fits into a value creation-e-management is different because doing it work requires the e-engineering of business eco-systems, e-management demands the ability to be connected to thousands of inputs about specific changes among many industry participants , such as suppliers , customers, employees, competitors, media and shareholders.

Effective e-management requires the ability to monitor developments that can change with unusually high frequency. However, it is also essential that e-managers distinguish between the few meaningful inputs and the many inputs that have limited significance, ability to sustain organizational change, effectie e-managers monitor changes in their markets. So, instead of e-commerce organizations need to employ talent e-managment staffs to help them to manage overall e-commerce organizations. E-leading staffs (HRM) is another main HRM need. E-leaders need to know how to design online brochures, e.g. online brochures simply involved putting a company's market materials on the web. in order to attract or persuade online buyers visit its websites and choose the most right price of product to buy easily. E-leaders need to lead front-office transactions which involved putting customer facing customers , such as placing on order on the web when leaving back-office activities, such as order fulfillment unchanged.

E-leaders also need to integrate online online purchase transactions in which a firm actually linked its front -office and back -office systems and processes in a fashion, e.g. most companies have developed online brochures , in order to let online advertisement tool to attract e-buyer individual purchase choice from its webstores. Hence, future any e-commerce organizations must need (HRM (e-leaders and e-managers) to help them to bring innovation in order to achieve maximize profit aim. So, internet webstores, e-leaders , e-managers may be future e-commerce organization main resources. So, e-commerce organizations, manages are actors at three levels: In the front line , as entrepreneurs, in the middle , as facilitators, and integrators, at the top as institution builders.

Hence, future new economical society, it creates e-commerce organizations number increases, when consumers began to accept online purchase transaction activities. Hence, it causes e-commerce began to feel internet (e-webstores, e-leaders, e-managers), they will be the most influential resources (intangible knowledge managment and tangible URM both resourcees to influence their success or failure.

● Why doe e-commerce organization believe (e-webstore design, e-leaders and e-managers) will be main organizational resources?

The most important question: It asks when e-buyers visit their webstores, wo are their target customers and shich needs of theirs are their trying to satisfy? For exap,e many airlines , e.g. American airlines, China airlines began to feel online e-tickets sale channel is more easily than paper ticket shop sale channel, because many air passengers began to accept e-ticket/online ticket purchase choice more than visiting airline shops . They feel that they do not want to waste time to visit airline shops. They like to pre-book to buy e-ticket to pay from the airline e-websote conveniently. Hence, e-webstore design knowledge management , e-leaders and e-management webstore management skill will be future any one e-commerce organizations their main tangible and intangible resources (assets) to help their e-commerce businesses development.

On conclusion, I believe that the current economy is not a high-tech economy or an internet economy, not an m-commerce economy , but instead customer econoomy. Customers need to gather with information and access, they are demanding, fair, global price, they are demanding that compares deal with them using the distribution channel , they choose manufacturing direct and through dealers and retailers. Base on those factors, they encourage future many e-commerce organizations cause organization change traditional resouce concept, such as land, capital equipment, tangible resource began to change to e-commerce organization's intangibel and tangible resource, such as knowledge management to e-online web store design skills, e-leaders and e-managers e-stores sale management strategy and e-buyer product research and brochure online advertisement design skill. All of these knowledge management skill will be future organizations' main resources to help them to create new economic competition effort.

Organization resources defination

What are organizational resources ? What do organizational resources mean? What kinds of organizational resources are needed? What negative impact may be influenced if organizations lack enough resources to influence organizational development? Does working time belong to organizational time resources to influence employee individual efficiency e.g. how arranging enough employee to do the identified task in the most short time in order to achieve the most efficient performane? I shall attempt to identify examples to explain above questions as below:

In general, organizational resources are all assets, that are available to a firm for use during the production process. The four basic types of organizational resources are human, monetary , raw materials and capital. Organizational resources are combined, used and transofrmed to finished products during the production process. For organizational human resource example, human resource activities full under the following five core functions: staffing, development, compensation, safety and health core functions.

● HR resource

HR conducts a wide variety of activities. However, in any organizations, the major resources used by organizations are often described as follow (1) human resources (2) financial respirces (3) physical resources and (4) information resources. Managers are responsible for acquring and managing the resources to accomplosh goals. Hence, in organizational HR aspect, it may include these function, such as retirement and selection, performance management , learning and development, succession planning, compensation and benefits, human resource information systems. Because considering that for many organizations employees themselves represent a significant cost to the business, if the organization can use its employees in efficiency.

Then, it can avoid human resource in excess or in surplus on wasting challenge. Then , its employee cost or salary can be reduced. I t means that it does not need to employ in excess employees number, but the organization can still achieve itself the most efficient performance. Hence, any organizations must need to learn how to avoid " in excess employees number supply or wasting employee working behaviors" challenge . Because if some tasks do not need many employees to work together, it can still be achieved efficiency . Then , the organization ought not employee too many or excess employees to finish the kind of task. Thus, learning how to use efficient human resources, it can help organizations to avoid wasting working time to any departments employees. For example, when one factory has limited land to be supplied to become warehouse in order to help it to keep sticks. If it has excess logistic or factory workers number. Then, they are wasting working time to do not important tasks in warehouse, it means that if the factory has only one warehouse, but its area is small, it can allow maximum 50 workers to stay in the warehouse , but the warehouse has above 100 workers are staying to deliver goods in the small warehouse . Then, they must not actieve the most efficiency , even their delivery or transport goods performance will be influenced to worse by noise and crowd warehouse working environment. Hence, excess employees number in any working environment, which can not improve organizational performance or riase efficiency any organizations can not neglect " excess employees number" organizatinal HR resource arranging issue.

The solution concerns arranging the most right or the most exact empllyees number in order to supply to any organizational departments. Then, the organization can avoid wasting employee individual talent, reducing employing cost, improvig performance, achieving the most efficiency. Resource capacity means resource pool who are available in the organization to take up to appropriate human resource arrangement to assist any departmental development in long term efficiency. Hence, organizational human rsources may become talent tangible assets or foolish tangible assets. It depends on how the organization's resource capacity tasks arrangement to every employee in different departments. If the organization neglects how to arrange every employee task in the most exact or the most appropriate employees number in the department.

The department's efficiency must be caused worse, because excess employees number, it can not help it to achieve the most efficiency aim, even it may influence the excess employees , themselves feel waste working hours to do the not essential or not important tasks. Then, the organization may cause talent employee to become foolish employee. Otherwise, the organization's efficiency to be worse, because when the department has not enough employees to work. Then , any one employee may feel hard to work, his/her emotion may be influenced to negative, then his/her workig behavior may b inefficiency or lazy working. On consequence, the organization may bring economic loss, due to employee individual lasy working behavior, negative working emotion, even high working pressure may be caused, when one employee needs to do more , then the employee's task, but his/her salary can not increase. He/she will feel unfair to compare the another department employee, he /she does not need to spend long working hours or overtime to work per day. SO, any organization needs to avoid shortage employee supply or excess employee supply issue to any departments. Appropriare employees number is the best strategy in order to raise overall organizational efficiency.

● Time resource

Instead of human resource, land, raw material, earth natural resource, electricity, gas may be organization resources . Whether time may be organizational resources, organizational time management vires time as a scarce resource that must be invested as effectivity. Time is an infinite resource . If not properly managed on in an organization. It can have a negative impact on both employer's and employee's productivity. So, organizations should ensure that workers are well equipped to manage time in their duties.So, in management view, any organization managers must need to consider how to manage time, eg . how to arrange employees to work in different departments in order to achieve the most efficiency. They need to understand which resources are in short supply and focus on the prioritizing work across shared resources, they need agree on a common approach, they also need to realize resource management is an ongoing process. Thus, time is an often ignored but invaluable resource in any organization. All activities be it procurement.

An organization's time, in contrast, goes largely unmanaged. Although, phone calls, email, instant messages , meetings, they are general daily tasks to any organizations managers, but mangers need to know how to arrange the most urgent tasks in prior. For example, if the manager can not arrange a meeting to the discuss client tomorroe, as well as the manager needs to spend two hours to meeting with overall 200 employees to discuss how to solve improving efficiency challenge tomorroe. So, this manager needs to make choice whether he ought spend two hours meeting to the business client, or two hours meeting to 200 employees. If he chooses to meet the business client tomorrow, he will help his firm to win the important business chance, but he can not discuss how to improve efficiency in order to find the best method to let 200 employees to know tomorrow. Thus, tomorrow time management will be one importat time resource to the manager. The manager needs to arrange tomorrow two hours time how to plan business meting or efficiency imporvement meerting either to his 200 employees or the one business client. Because if the manager decided to meet the client, he must need to spend today time to aplan or organize how to arrange either business proposal content for the business client or organizational operational challenge questions and solutions for his 200 employees . So, today time management is also important time resource to influence tomorrow either the success business meeting or the organizational 200 employees meeting. So, it seems that time management may be one important resource to any managers more than general employees in any organizations.

If the manager can know how to manager his/her time to do any prior tasks, then he/she may help the organization to raise efficiency or improve performance. Otherwise, if the manager can not know how arrange what prior urgent task needs to be finished. Then, worse performance or inefficiency may be influenced to cause. So, if the organization manager can know how to make time arrangement, I believe that he can help the organization employees to raise efficiency more easily.

Organization efficient using resources economic method
In behavioral economic view , any organizations can attempt to apply behavioral economy method to use resources efficiently. Organizational excellence framework performance measurement takes a systematic approach . One of the most effective ways of using resources and minimizing that use of work. Calculating task cost in the most efficient economic method to help organizations to reduce cost and avoid resources waste, e.g. using resource management software, technology, planning and taking a systematic approach , which aims to manage the most efficient steps to follow to finish or implement each task in the most shor time as well as avoiding excess employees number.
Organizational resource efficiency means using the organization's limited resources in a sustainable manner when minimising impacts on the organization performance. It allows the organization to create more with less and to deliver greater value with less money. HR, raw material, technology input to carry on any organizational resources efficiently ? Management is the process of using organizational resources to achieve organizational goals of using organizational resources to achieve organizational

goals effectively and efficiently through planning , organizing , leading and controlling. An efficient organization makes the most productive use of its resource in the most short time and the most eficiency and the least cost aspects.

● What is efficient use of resources to any organizations in economics?

Economic efficiency implies an economic state in which every resource is optimially allocated to serve each individual or entity in the best way when minimizing waste and inefficiency. whan an economy is economically efficient, any changes made to assist one entity would harm another . Hence, budget how much spending on resources, e.g. employee saley, office and/or plant technological equipment facilities , before making resource expenditure spending decision. Budget is essnetial to help the organization to deduce resource using and excess purchase waste since budget and resource of organizations have interlock or interconnet relationship. If the organization can make exact udget, then it can avoid excess expenditure or waste resource to use. So, organizations need to acquire a talented resource pool , that can lead projects to success, when any kinds of resources are achieved to be supplied to use inn enough . For example, using an effective enterprise resource management system that delivers capabilities. Regardless of the approach and tools used, organizations must determine how to balance to use any kinds of resources efficiently. Thus, in organizational efficient resource using behavioral economy view, the organizational efficiency factor means that influences the efficiency of the organization's use if its resources can be both internal and external, e.g. how implementing strategic plans, they may include selecting what methods and resources to use, and leadning employees on guideline, working in coalitions with organizations around to deliver those needs in the most resource efficient way.

In organizational studies, resource managemetn is the efficient and one resource management technique of resource leveling, of finding the answers to the question, how to use available resource efficiently, effectively and economically ot organization resource expense. SO , resource management is the process of allocating resources and allocating.

● What is meant by economic using of resource to organizations?

Economic resources are the factors used in producing goods or providing services. Economic resources can be divied into human resources, such as labors and management, and non humann resource, such as land, capital , goods, finished resources and technology , for example, natural resource is a key input in the production process that stimulates economic growth. Natural resources have limited direct economic use in satisfying human need, but transforming them into goods and services enhances their economic value to the socirty. So, if the country has many organizations know how to use their natural resources input in that production processes. Then, they can create themselves economic benefits directly and attribute economic benefit to society indirectly.

Thus, the types of economic organizations can be identified, there are subsistence recipreocal exchange with subsistence, peasant with primary reliance on self-produced food, but containing some exhange elements, market-commercial , redistribution or state socialist. Thus organizations need to learn hoe to use themselves organizational resources efficiently. Organizational resources are all assets that are to a firm for use during the production process. The four basic types of organizational resources are human, monetary, raw material and capital. Organizational resources are combined , used and transformed into finished products during the production process. So, a business that understands how to use resources efficiently. resource management is the process of allocating resources in order for a company to grow easily.

Organizational economic is used to study transactions within individual firms and determine management approach to managing resources. It is broken down into thee major subjects: agency theory, transaction cost economic and property rights theory. Agency theory is a priinciple that is used to explain and resolve issues in the relationship between business principles and their agents. Most commonly, that relationship is the one between shareholders as principles, and company executives as agents. Agency theory is used to understand the relationship between agents and principals. The agent represents the principal in a particular business transaction and is expected to represent the best interests of the principal without regard for seld interest. So, when the relationship between shreholders and company executives is kept the best.

Transaction cost economic is understood as alternative modes of organizing transactions (governance structure, such as markets, firms and bureaus) that mininize transactions costs. This, cost is the primary determinant of such as firm's decision whether it is the most right (the best) or the worst decision. It will influence the firm ho to spend resource behavior. The cost other than the money price that are incurred in trading good and service. SO, if the organization can often make the best decision to carry on any activites. It will avoid to waste resources efficiently. For example, if transaction cost influces the commission, paid to a stockbroker for completing a share deal and booking fee charges when purchase concert tickets. The cost of travel and time to complete an exhange , it means that transaction cost. So if the organization can make the best or the most reasonable decision to carry on any business activities. Then, its transaction cost can be influenced to reduce the most level in order to bring resources economic benefit. e.g. sunk costs are indpeendent of any event and should not resulting from economic trade in a market.

Property right theory means contracted choice, through ownership, property rights theour clarifies the firm's boundary choice. The maon egal property rights are the right of possession, the righ tof excession. So, for the efficiency of property rights al scarce resources are owned by someone. IN the right property rights approsed to the theory of the firm, I assume that in the case of sale ownership by party-property rights define the theoretical and legal ownership of resources and how resources can be used by organizatin. So, above three major organizational theories can assist organizations to know how to spend resources efficiently.

The relationship between organization resources using and social resources

Resources needers may include societies needers ,e.g. government house material householders , electricity , water , natural resources needers, schools, public houses

, land number and area needs etc. as well as business organiztions , office building material, office, plant, land area, number need, equipment facilities limited number . So, when global office and plant business users need to buy more land, equipment materials etc. and electricity , water. Social resources number reduces to bring resourcee shortage challenge causes. Have they have shortage relationship (resource demand number is more than supply number) between social resources need and business resource need? I shall attempt to explain this question as below:

I assume global business organization number increases, they will need many natural resources, e.g. water, electricity, gas, land to supply for office, plant building , material and staff office electricity, gas, plant , office daily essential power need. So, when global business organizations number increases, they may need to use much raw material and natural resources for equipment facility, office plant building material, even day office, plant electricity , gas power, staff drinking water etc. basic office operational needs, when global business organizations number increase.

The question concerns whether they will cause natural resources shortage to supply to social need , when global business organizatins number increases. First, I shall explains what social resources needers mean as below:

● Social resource are defined as any concrete or symbolic term that

can be used as an object of exchange among people (Foa & Foa, 1980), money, information, goods and services both tangible items , such as are ususally defined the assessment of social need is of central allocation between organization needers and social citizen needers both stakeholders. So, when global human birth rate and life time increases, population number will increase, then their social resources need are also increasing, if global organizaions and population number are increasing in the same time, due to earth natural resources has limit number to supply in order to satisfy organizations and families daily resources need, e.g. building material resources are used to build either to build offices, plants or private houses , public house, lands resources are used either to build private or public houses or offices , plants , water is supplied to either office staffs drinking or families drinking, electricity , gas resources are limited to supply either offices plants use or families private or public houses use. Hence, due to all of earth, but in the same time, global offices , plants, government organizations and families numbers both stakeholders number is continue increasing. They have possible to encounter natural resources shortage issue when natural resources are using much, but they can nt manufacturers to increase by human easily.

● Can responding to resource scarcity help some kinds business grow?

Foe example, the food and agricultural business organizations, e.g. supermarkets, restaurants, they must send plactic material to manufacture plactic bags to supply to supermarket buyers to carry fruits, breads, mil, etc. foods when consumers need to buy the kinds of foods in any supermarkets, if plactic material supply number is decreasing, then a lot plactic bags can not supply to let buyers to carry their foods, due to plactic bags number is shortage , it will cause any supermarket buyers feel inconvenient when they need plactic bags to carry their foods, they choose to buy the kind of foods from supermarket to themselves homes.

So, if plactic bags manufacture material i shortage, it can not be manufactured to plactic bags to supply to global supermarket organizations. Then, the one supermarket can provide enough plactic bags to let them to carry their foods from supermarkets to themselves homes conveniently. The focus on plactic bag resource scareity is not impossible to occur to supermarket organization case. If families are often using plactic bag to carry rubbish daily at home. Then, plactic bags number can not increase to satisfy global supermarkets food plactic bags and families themselves homes rubbish plactic bags both stakeholders need. Plastic bags can not be manufactured to supply to manufacture lot plactic bags supply to satisfy global families rubbish plactic bags home users and supermarkets food plactic bas users needs. Consequently, plactic bags prices may be influenced to increases, when plactic bags demand increases, but supply decreases. It is one good exaple to explain why plactic bag manufacturered material supply decreases, it may influence plactic bags number decreases and price increases, because families home rubbish plactic bags and supermarket food plastic bags need both increase.

Consequence, supermarket cost may be influenced , due to plastic bags number also increase much, if one day shortage of plactic manufacturing material supply number is shortage. So, it seems that food plastis bags using number, they have close relationship to impact supermarket food plastic bags price, if supermarkets lack enough plastic bag number supplies, then they need to increase food price, even the supermarket may lose customers , if it can not supply plastic bags to let them to use the supermarket itself plastic bags to carry fruits, ,ilk, soft drinks conveniently.

Hence, plastic bag material may be one kind of important natureal resource for supermarkets, because any one consumer may be influenced to choose another supermarket when he/she feels the another supermarket can supply plastic bags to let him/her to carry on fruits, milks, soft drinks conveniently.

Another kind of natureal resource , such as steel material for restaurants , steel material can help global restaurants to manufacture kniefs, glass sups for restaurants customers to eat food or drink , if much steels are used to manufactured cars product to satisfy car drivers' driving lesiure need , then it may also influence restaurants s' knieves, glass cups price increases, due to cost increase, restaurants need to increase food price to compensate its knief, glass cups price. even, many families feel need to buy many gloass cups to drink water, then it may also influence global glass cups price increase. If one day steel material is shortage , this kind of natural resource must influence restaurants glass cups , knief cost increases. So, their general food price may be influenced to increase. It is not fair to global restaurants food consumers.

Hence, it explains resource shortage may influence some kinds of business cost increases, as well as consumer foods, products services price increases. It means that " resource shortage may influence some kinds of businesses cost increases".

In fact, in our societies, natural resource shortage may influence any kinds of business cost increases, w.g. car manufacturing industry, if one day stell manufacturing material is shortage. it will cause many car manufacturers can not buy enough steels to manufacture cars. When, global car buyers number increases, but global cars number can not increase rapidly, due to steel material can not supply enough. Then, cars prices may be influenced to raise. SO, it seems that steel resource shortage may bring reasonable chance to let global car manufacturers to raise cars prices. When , global car buyes ' new car purchase needs are increasing, hence, natural resource shortage may influence some kinds of business produce prices increase in possible, when the kind of product , such as many people begin to chose to buy new cars, more than second hand cars. The, when steel material supplies shortage, it may influence new car price increases in global can market.It means that any organizations ought not waste natural resource. Otherwise, it may influence their cost increases.

Environmental resource scarcity would likely have been adaptivve in the human evolitionary parst, resources in the environment and organization resource shortage problem might alsoo effect how satisfied they were. Hence, organizations in virtually every industry face the challenge of new managing resources effectively. The influence would run the other way instability as rival, such as big data platforms for e-commerce organizations, e.g. e-book publishers, online sellers. Big data platforms lift limitations on the size of computing resources that can be applied for data, in other words, data storage and e-commerce organizations can significantly influence computing efficiency.

Hence, organizational resources may also influence computer industry information gathering intangible resources, if the electronic books publish, or online electronic commerce product sellers can gather the most up-date consumer individual purchase behavioral data in short time daily rapidly. Then, they collect the most accurate electronic books readers or the kind of online product buyers past purchase choice in order to judge whther which topics of books are the most popular or which kinds of product to the most popular to let them to implement sale strategy, e.g. whether which topic of e-books prices need to be increased ot decreased, whether which kinds of products prices need to be increases or decreased. So, the big data gathering speed is the technology resource to e-commerce market organizations.

III

Amazon ecommerce organization resource useful strategy

Management accounting science how applies to Amazon ecommerce organization

Management accounting concept can help organizations to do management budget strategies, e.g. margin analysis, capital budget, inventory valuation and product cost budget, trend analysis and forecast . Management accounting also called managerial accounting or cost accounting, is the process of analysis business costs and operations to prepare internal financial report, records and managers decision making process in achieving business goals.

However, management accountants depend on standard financial statements containing the earning statement, cash flow statement and balance sheet. In addition , it also makes use of additional finds reports in analysizing the information of the organization including budget performance and cost reports. I shall attempt to explain how management account science can help organizations to analyze cost , why and how changes in order to avoid expense increases or excess cost cases or loss increases.

For Amazon e-commerce publish organization example, Amazon publish is a famous publish organization. It applies internet (online) channel to help authors to sell electronic books and paper books to different countries readers. It also cooperate to other publishers to deliver any its anthors books to their webstores, so when one reader chooses its publish partner webstores to buy Amazon any author books, then Amazon publish will share royalty income between them. Hence, Amazon publish may be book distribution partner to its other e-publish partners.

● How management accounting cocept can help Amazon publish to manage its cost effectively in order to increase its profit or e-books or paper books sale ability.

Amazon publish is a e-comerce organization. It depends high internet speed to help global authors to register Amazon publish's individual author account , then any global authors may download their book files to produce any ebooks and papers to sell from Amazon publisher webstores as wellas global any readers can apply Amazon publish webstores to buy any author individual paper or ebooks from its web-publish stores rapidly. So, Amazon publish must need have fast speed internet technology to support its books sale ability,

It brings this question: How much does Amazon publish internet expenditure need? Does it need to pay shops rent per month? Because Amazon publish has none any actual book shops to locate in any countries. So, Amazon publish must not pay rent to any countries for its shops. Although Amazon publish does not need to pay rent for any book shops, but Amazon publish needs to pay extra internet expenditure to US internet service provider to support its electronic webstores daily electronic books and paper books every purchase transaction, any countries author individual book electronic files download per day 24 hours . So, Amazon publish must need to pay more expenditure for internet service to support its authors and readers their electronic books and paper books purchase and sale transaction per day 24 hours.

As Amazon publish case, in its financial report indicates , it does not pay any book stores rent expenditure or book stores (shops) building building expediture on its profit and loss account, but Amazon publish must need to pay internet service expenditure to US internet service provider. Moreover, this internet service expenditure must be more amount, due to it needs to provide its webstores online book (electronic books and paper books) to sell and electronic library e-book lending service to global readers, 24 hours. Thus, internet service expenditure must be Amazon publish long-term influential transaction expenditure because, any electronic books and paper books, even e-library books borrow service and readers must need to pay visa card for borrowing book month service fee and purchase books from amazon publish e-publish webstores in any time every day.

Hence, Amazon publish must need have good management

account strategy in order to predict whether different countries will have how many readers click to its different countries e-publish webstores to spend time to choose different authors books to buy or borrow to read from intenet channel. So, any countries readers budgeting number, readers reading habit behavior, e.g. US has about one million online readers click Amazon e-publish webstores , but it has only three thousands readers pay visa card to buy its ebooks and paper books from its Amazon electronic publish webstores, in this week , but next week, US has about seven thousands online readers click Amazon e-publish webstores, but it has three thousands readers pay visa card to buy its ebooks and paper books. Hence, it seems tha although this week has one million online readers click to Amazon publish electonic webstores to seek any books, but the book buyer number has only three thousands. Otherwise, although next week, it reduces three thousands e-readers click to visit Amazon e-publish webstores e-readers number , but it still keep same three thousand e-readers to choose to buy Amazon publish's books to read.

I assume that Amazon publish needs to pay a fixed internet service expenditure, e.g. US $500,000, but it design this e-publish webstores can help it to do its different countries e-publish webstores, their daily e-readers visiting number, daily electronic book and paper book sale number and daily e-readers visiting time statistics. It's electronic publish webstores can help it to record any countries' reading habits and reading taste , e.g. how many fiction , story books have sold in the week, how many non fiction books have sold in the week , e.g. business topic books have sold next week.

So, Amazon publish can use its e-publish webstores to gather above data in order to make author book topic sale choice, e.g. whether this week, US market ought sell how many consumer psychological topic book, US market ought sell how many management topic book next week. If this week US market can only sell one thousand consumer psychological topic book to compare its budget is less than one thousand consumer psychological topic books budget sale number reduces, e.g. in the week, there are two thousands readers choose to buy consumer psychological topic books from European market in this week. It implies that there are many European readers who like to read consumer behavior books recently. Hence, Amazon can attempt to concentrate on encouraging authors to write more consumer psychological books to let European readers to read within next several months.

Basic on above effects, Amazon needs to provide rapid internet service to European libraries, schools ,e-book partners to help them to promote Amazon consumer psychology topic books in order to let the European consumer psychological students, consumer psychology lecturers, consumer psychologists to know Amazon publish can provide more different topics concern consumer psychology research in order to increase Amazon 's consumer psychology book European market book buyers bumber.

As above case, I assume Amazon publish needs to pay a fixed internet service expenditure , e.g. US$500,000 per month. Amazon needs webstores to evaluate whether it is value, if it helps European schools, libraries organizations to pay internet fee, in order to let they can let many consumer psychology students and teachers and consumer psychologists to know that Amazon publish may have enough different consumer psychology books to be provided to European publish libraries, schools readers to read. For example, I assume next several month, Amazon publish needs to pay US two million internet service expenditure to global different European countries to help Amazon publish itself to promote its al different authors' consumer psychology topic books as well as it evaluates that it will sell different European countries; students , teachers and consumer psychologists readers, they have about three million readers at least choose to buy its one million consumer psychology topic authors; paper books and electronic books next several months as well as it also needs to evaluate whether it can earn more than US ten million at least royalty income after reducing author royalty from all European countries book markets.

Thus, if Amazon publish makes decision to help European countries schools, public libraries to pay internet expenditure to help it to advertise its one million consumer psychology topic authors electronic and paper books to sell. It must needs to pay fixed US$500,000 internet expenditure for Amazon publish its all e-bpublish webstores and it also needs to pay extra two million internet service expenditure for global all European countries libraries and schools per month. If next month, Amazon publish can earn more than US tem million at least royalty income after reducing author royalty from all European countries book market. Then, Amaozn publish ought attempt to make this internet service expenditure for all European schools, libraries organizations, if it had confidence to earn this royalty amount from European consumer psychology book readers, such as this Amazon publish.

On conclusion, , this Amazon publish organization case, it may attempt to apply management accounting science method to make book sale number budget, royalty income budget, even analysis to reader individual reading habit, book topic choices, book sale price evaluation in order to judge whether the kind or topic book ought concentrates on selling to which countries marekts, such as Amazin publish case, it also may choose different consumer psychology topic books to concentrate on selling to different European countries in next several months, if it can earn all European royalty income more than its internet service expenditure to European schools, libraries, then Amazon may attempt to make this decision. Otherwise, it won't be good decision. Hence, it implies that management accounting is one kind of business management science, it can apply number to help any organizations to do right or reasonable reason more accurate as well as it is different to traditional financial acounting, it only helps organizations to record and income and expenditure, earn or loss record function. Hence, management accounting may help any organizations to attempt implement useful or effective strategies in order to improve themselves performance.

How management accounting concept applies to investment

Can we apply management accounting concept to investment decision aspect? An organization's investment decision may make risk, so they need risk evaluation to decide whether the project can bring ehat benefit before they want any decisions. Risk management is the process of assessing, managing and mitigating losses . This applies to both business and investing risk management exists in many forms throughout the financial world, such as one individual investor decides to buy low risk government securities, instead of high yield corporate bonds in an example of risk managment companies and investors frequently use financial managment method like options, and future and strategies, like portfolio and investment diversification, in order to effectively manage risk.

For investment management strategy example, it is professional asset management of various securities, including shareholdings, bonds and other assets, such as real estate, in order to meet specified investment goals for the benefits of investors. Investors may be insurance companies, pension funds, corporations, charities, educational organizations or private invetors.

The term asset management is often used to refer to the management of investment funds. So managerial accounting is the process of identifications, measurement , analysis and interpretation of accounting information that helps business leaders make financial decisions and efficiently manage their day operation . The main objective of managerial accounting is to maximize profit and minimize losses . It is concerned with the presentation of data to predict inconsistencies in finances that help managers make important decisions, such as investment decision for Amazon publish book sale country market choice for which topic of books which are the most popular, in order to concentrate on selling the topic of books to the country market. So, Amazon publish needs to gather past different kinds for any one country, number data may include each author ebook and paper books sale prices, each author different book topic books sale number , in order t make which topic of book sale to which countries investment decision aims to increase readers number t o the country book sale market. So, Amazon publish may be apply these tools of management accounting to gather datas to concern book sale record. They may include: Financial accounting, financial statement analysis, book cost accounting, fund flow analysis , cash flow analysis, standard costing, marginal cost, budgetary control , management accounting tools.

● How to apply mental accouting method to predict investor behavior?

The main aim of management accounting to investment includes planning, controlling and evaluating. Thus, the advatanges to investment may include; better decision making, increase business efficiency, simplify financial statement, raises profitability, motivates employees, cost control, reliability. Hence, management accounting means " mental accouting", it is a concept in the field of behavioral economies. Mental accouting refers to the different values of person places on the same amount of money, based on subjective criteria, often with detrimental results. Mental accouting is a concept in the field of behavioral economies. Developed by economist Richard H, it contends that individuals classify funds differently and therefore are prone to irrational decision making in their spending and investment behavior. It refers to the different values people value on money, based on subjective criteria, that often has detrimental results, mental (managerial)accounting decisions and behave in financially counterproductive or detrimental ways, such as funding a low interest savings account when carrying learge credit card balances, to avoid the mental (managerial) accounting bias, individuals should treat money as perfectly used tools when they allocate among different accounts, be it a budget account (everyday living expenses), a spending account or a wealth account (saving and investment). Also abother author indicates that managerial accounting means mental accounting, which appeared in the Journal of behavioral decision making, the begins with this definition, " mental accounting" is the set of lognitive operations used key individuals and households to organize, evaluate , and keep tracks of financial activities. He considers of how mental accounting leads to irrational spending and investment behavior.

● How mental (managerial) accounting concept helps Amazon publish to make investment decision?

I believe that Amazon publish may apply mental accounting concept to help it to predict whether which topic of books will be the most popular to sell to the country market more accurately. The reason concerns that it can apply all data gathering to analyze whether past has how many readers paid visa to buy the topic of electronic or paper books to prepare to the country , e.g. in this year, Jan. it had 40,000 readers buy fiction electronic books and paper books from Amazon publish US market website to read , it had 100,000 readers buy fiction electronic and paper books to read in European market website and the year Feb. It had 70,000 readers paper books from Amazon publish US market website, it had 200,000 and paper books from Amazon publish European market website. Now, it is Mar. So, Amazon publish may make assumption that fiction (story) topic book is accepted to read by American and European readers, due to US fiction readers had increased 30,000 number in past one month and European fiction readers had increased 100,000 number in past one month.

However, US and European readers number data is not enough to evaluate whether US and European fiction readers number may still keep to increase. It depends on other factors, e.g. fiction e-book and fiction paper book sale price, if one author's ficton's ebooks and paper books rising prices whether it will influence US and European fiction book buyers make book purchas decision to the author's any fictions. So, Amazon publish need s to make the author's past different kinds of fiction books sale prices record in order to judge whether his fiction book's variable price (changing price) will bring negative or positive impact to his readers' fiction book purchase decision. For exmaple, if the author (A)'s one fiction price increased 10% to ebook and paper book sale price between Jan and Feb. His fiction readers number won't be influenced to reduce, even his fiction readers number can still increase 10%. So, it implies that this author's fiction is attract or popular to US and Eurpopean fiction reader market. Amazon publish ought concentrate on helping this author (A) to advertise his fiction to let many US and European readers to know.Hence, it explains that Amazon publish may attempt to gather past every author individual writing book topic book sale proce whether it is increased or decreased how much %, book sale number in order to make book sale investment decision to concentrate on helping whom to advertise to sell to which book sale country market.

So, it seems that mental accounting concept can be applied to Amazon publish to help it to do any author individual book sale country market advertisement investment decision. For example, if Amazon publish can only spend US$10,000 advertieing expenditure to help author (A) to sell fictions to US and European both markets in Mar. , then it can help author (A) to increase 20% more fiction sale number to US and European both markets. This advertisement expenditure is worth to spend for this author (A) in fiction market.

Hence, it implies that mental accounting concept can be applied to publish investment market, such as choosing which country to sell which topic of books, e.g. US sells more which fiction or European sells more fiction or Japan sells more management business topic books or UK sells more consumer psychology business topic books. All of these issues will be any publisher's important book sale market decision . It may influence their royalty income because if the publisher makes wrong decision to sell not popular topic books to the country market, e.g. in the month, US ought have many business topic readers to choose any business topic books to buy from any publishers, if the publisher makes wrong decision to find many fiction authors to help it to increase fiction stock to prepare to sell to US book market. Then, excess fiction stock may cause low fiction price (fiction book supply or publisher's fiction stock number) is more than fiction book demand (readers). Otherwise, it can not increase business topic books royalty inocme to US book market, because it has not enough different topic, such as management, consumer psychology , accounting, economy , marketing topic business books stock to be putted on book shelves to let US readers to choose when they visit US any book shops in the month.

On conclusion, it explains why mental (managerial) accounting has close relationship to influence customer behavior in behavioral economy view. Mental accounting is a management science or behavioral science tool to help any businessmen to make the most effective or the most reasonable busines decision in nowadays society.

Management science accounting concept how predicts market changing

Accounting aims to help any organizations to record whether the year has what kinds of expenditures, how much of every kind of expenditure finds what factors to cause the kind of expenditure needs to be spent too much in order to avoid excess spending, measurement profict or loss level why what factors cause the year had loss or profit growth in order to achieve long term performance improvement or avoiding loss. Hence, accounting system is not only for bookkeeping record financial performance aim. Accoungint may be one kind management science concept to be applied to explain why and how market changes in order to predict whether the company ought implement which strategies to grow up its business groth or increase clients number.

The question concerns why the organization can apply accounting concpet to predict how the market will change in order to avoid profit falls down or loss causes. I shall attempt to explain as below:

For a watch product sale organization example, this watch sale compay own 100 expensive price watch brand products stock to prepare to sell, their sale prices are between US\$3,000 to US\$5,000 , so the watch brand prices are below than US\$3000, they belong to low prices. It has 100 low price watch brand products stock to prepare to sell. Hence, every month, it keeps exact 100 high price of brand watch products stock and exact 100 low price of brand watch products stoc to prepare to sell. I assume this watch company can sell 100 low price watches and 100 high price watches in this month, but next month, it can sell 50 low price watches and 0 high price watches. Hence, it means that next watch , low prices watches sale number falls 50 number and high price watches sale numbe falls 100 number. It ensures that this company's profit may be influenced to fall by the high and low watch price client reducing number factor. However, this company still lacks data to know whether its competitors ; watch price is the main factor to influence its watch buyers number reduces or whether other factors influence its watch buyers number reduces, e.g. whether its high and low watchs are attractive or not attractive to high its watch design buyers number reduces or whether smart phone product invention influences watch users begin feel watchs have not be importnt to help them, because smart phones have time record function, they can replace traditional watch products or this month has higher unemployment rate, so it causes people do not like spend easily , in special, watch is not one kind essential product. Hence, it seems that this watch company can investigate its every month whether its low and high price watch stock sale record in order to attempt tp find whether what are the main factor to cause its watch sale number increases or decreases? I shall follow above every possible points to be investigated by accounting concept in order to explain why its watch low and high price customer number sudden reduces.

I assume that this watch company's last month and this month every high and low price watch brand's sale prices are stable. So, it seems that the influential factor won't be its " increasing sale price" to cause its high and low watch price customers number sudden reduces. If it gathered data concerns its watch competitots similar famous watch brands of general price range. It discovered their general sale prices do not have much difference between itself and their famous brnad of watchs. Also, it discovered that their these famous brand high and low price watch sale number is more than its sale number, e.g. the another similar famous watch brand company can sell 200 high price watchs and 200 low price watchs last month and 400 high price watchs and 400 low prcice watch this month. So, it seems that its high and low price of watch is not main factor to influence its watch sale number, because its high and low price watch's their price level had not changeed within these two months . Moreove, its watchs manufacture material costs had not increased within these two months. So, it ensures that its profit falls must not be influenced by watch manufacture cost increasing factor. Hence, it may depends on its accounting record to conclude the main factors influence its high and low price watch sale number reduces, they may include; poor watch design feeling to watch buyers factor, smart phones increasing need factor, unemploymenr rate rising factor.

The next step concerns how this watch company can apply accounting concept to find whether the main factor is poor watch design feeling factor, or smart phones are popular accepted to replace watch product feeling factor, or rising unemployment rate factor which one influences it s high and low price range watch sale number decreases can apply accounting cencept to investigate which is the main factor to influences its watch sale number decreased in this two months? I shall attempt to confirm this possibility as below: Firstly, I assume this watch company's accounting record has marketing promotion expenditure, its expenditure includes advertisement fee, exhibition expense only, however, in its expenditure group accounting record, it has none design expenditure with these two months. Hence, it seems that its high and low price range fanous brands watches had not been improved by its improvement design skill method in order to improve their watch style, picture, shape, colour, function , design to satisfy watch buyers'changing watch fashion need in this competitive market. Hence, it seems that poor watch design feeling factor may be one main factor to influence its watch sale number decreases. It implies that accounting record may help it to find lacking new fashion watch design factor may be one main influential factor to cause watch buyers choose to buy other similar famous brands' watch products.

Next, whether accounting concept can help this firm to judge whether smart phones influences its watch sale number? I assume that smart phone products had been selling more than 10 years in this country in this case indicates US country. So, smart phones mus be its long time similar time seeing function competitors in US. I assume that its past 10 years high and low price range famous brand watches sale number must be more than these two months as well as it had not increases high and low price range of watches prices within this 10 years. Hence, it can depend on its past 10 years accounting record to judge whether smart phones product invention may influence watch buyers number decreases within these two months. basic on its past 10 years , accouniting record indicated that its high and lw price range watch sale number had been increasing, and it s watch price had not beedn increased and its markting advertisement promotion expense had been reducing much within 10 years. Thus, its past watching expense and watch price sale amount and profit accounting record may help it to conclude that smart phone product sale to US market is not the main factor to influence its recent high and low price range watchs sale number falls.

Finally, I shall explain whether this watch company may apply accounting concept to explain whether this month's high unmployment rate factor can influence geeral watch buyers' consumption desire as below:

I assume that this watch company employed 20 watch salespeople and their salaries range are between US$2,000 to US $4,000 per month in the first years . It operated till to this month total 20 years . However, its accounting record indicated that its watch salespeople number had been increasing from 20 to 50 number recently and their salaries range had been increading between US$3,000 to US$6,000 permonth. Hence, within these 10 years , this watch company employees number and their salaries range had been continue increasing. . It may depend on its past 10 years accounting record for salespeople salaries and employee number to reflect whether higher unemployment rate is the main factor to influence its watch sale number reduces.

I assume that within these 10 years, its unemployment rare was between 1% to 10%, in US society , although it may had 1% to 10% young people unemployed within 10 years. But, this watch company, I could also increased salespeople employees number and their salaries could also increase more significantly, even their salaries had not decreased in these 10 years. Hence, its accounting record of salsepeople salaries increasing trend , it may reflect this US watch market's local and overseas watch buyer individual buying watch desires ought not be influenced by slight rising unemployment rate factor, it is based on that this watch company will like to increase salespeople employee number, when it discovered there were many potential watch buyers visited its any watch shops every day within past 10 years. Hence, it implies higher unemployment rare won't influence watch potential buyer individual visiting to any one watch shops in US within these 10 years. So, this watch company's past salespeople salaries, employees number, and their salaries rising range record can reflect whether US higher unemployment ratio level can influence its recent high and low price range of watchs sale number decreases in US local watch sale market.

On conclusion, we can depend this watch company past 10

years accounting record to judge whether which one may be the most main fluential factor to influence its recent watch sale number reduces. I make the final conclusion that its poor watch design feeling factor ought be its main factor to influence its recent watch sale number reduces, due to it had not spend any design expenditure to improve its watch style in order to attract many watch buyers' choices within these 10 years. So, I believe that accounting concept can help any companies to revise whether what factos influence their businessess to be better or worse, instead of general booking record function.

Accounting trademark loyalty theory

In accounting theory view, any organizational goodwill or trademark, they are intangible asset because they can not touch, they are the company name. However, when the organization grows up a long time, ususally more than 10 years, if they are famous when consumers choose to buy the kind of product, they will must remember, then the organization's trademark or goodwill, company names will become the company's intangible asset in their balance sheet , financial report, e.g. Cock Coke soft drink, " Coca Coke" may be this soft drink company's trademaek , intangible asset to this soft drink company. Because any country's soft drinkers, they must remember Coca Coke brand soft drink before they make any brands of soft drink purchase choice. The reason may be Coca Coke soft drink . Its brand had been popular to be accept to be the first soft drink choice to any countries people. Hence, Coca Coke soft drink compnay must put is brand name to be intanginle asset in balance sheet, (B/S),

Why does Coca Coke's brand name (intangible asset) value may increase or decrease in B/S. The reason is simple, when general consumers feel Coca Coka drink has better taste to compare other brands soft drinks. Then, they wil choose other brand soft driks to replace Coca Coke soft drink. So, if the year, Coca Coke's any taste of soft drinks sale number decreases, then it will feel its intangible asset of trademark value is devaluation, but if its soft drink sale number increases in this year. Its intangible asset of trademark value will increase in its B/S.

Hence, it explains why Coca Coke 's trade mark value can reflect its soft drink sale number whether it increases or decreases in the year. Thus, any firms mist hope their trademark , goodwill valuation can often increase every year. The question concerns how they can often keep their trademark valuation to increase? Can the firm increase sale number , it can represent that it has long term goodwill valuation increases? Can other factors influence or impact the firm's goodwill valuation changes? I shall attempt to give examples to explain these questions as below:

In fact, goodwill or trademark represents the company's famility whether how many consumers can remember its brand name , when they choose to buy the kind of product . So, if the firm's products are famous in market, Its products must have many consumers can remember it before they choose to buy the kind of product. So, product's familiar to publish,which ill be one measurement tool to judge whether what may be its goodwill valuation. If there are many consumers remember its brand before they want to buy the kind of products, the firm ought raise its goodwill valuation. It may make market research to enquire whether consumer will choose to buy which brand of product among several similar brands of product. It many people choose to prefer to buy its brand. Then, its brand familiar level to publis will be high grade. It may raise to goodwill valuation inB/S.

So, I think that goodwill fact valuation can not be measured by sale number or sale price or profit or loss amount. It ought be measured by market familiar level. If the product can have many people know its brand exitence in market. Then, its goodwill , intangible asset valuation ought be increased. Otherwise, if there are not may people know or they are familiar its brand existence in market. Then, its probable valuation ought need to decrease . Hence, any firms' goodwill valuation ought reflect their market familiar level for standard.

Do you feel firm goodwill valuation can represent its market value or product sale effort? In accounting principle, goodwill valuation must be measured by money. For example, Coca Coke brand goodwill valuation, in fact, Coca Coke had not pay another in B/S. Its goodwill valuation increases, it is not due to it pays its firm pays cash to buy goodwill. It is due to its capital increase. But, in fact, it does not need to increase cash to capital balance amount in B/S. Because coca Coke has not increase its cash amount, due to goodwill valuation increases. Its goodwill valuation increases, it supposes that is capital amount also be influenced to increase. So, Coca Coke 's goodwill valuation can not represent it has profit growth. Goodwill valuation only represents it has profit growth. Goodwill valuation only represents Coca Coke's present market valuw whether it increases or decreases in soft drink market. It is not actual cash available value. So, why firms need have goodwill valuation. The reason is simple. If one day, the firm hopes to sell its busines to another. When the another potential business buyer feels this firm's goodwill valuation is high. It may persuade b make business purchase decision more easily. because he believes that there are many people are famkliar this product brnad , then they will choose to buy theis product in preference . So, good goodwill valuation can build good business sale image to help the firm can raise business sale price to anyone . Such as Coca Coke soft drink goodwill case, if it can keep high goodwill valuation, then it can persuade any businesses buyers accept to pay high business purchase price. so, B/S goodwill valuation may help any famous business to sell to anyone in the high business sale price more easily.

Can goodwill valuation help the firm to predict market environment changes? For Coca Coke soft drink case example, I assume that it estimated its goodwill valuation is US 3 million , but this year, it estimates its goodwill valuation falls down to US one million. What factors influence Coca Coke feels its goodwill valuation reduces US two million in this year? I believe that is current year goodwill valuatin falls, it has relationship to whole global soft drink taste changes to global soft drinkers. The factors influence global drink makes taste changes , they may include: global soft drinkers begin to dislike to choose to drink any brands of soft drink in preference, if they feel soft drink is one kind of bad health drink. They may choose to buy freash fruits to eat to replace any soft drink. I assume that the other soft drink brand companies' goodwill valuations are decrased. It means that if other soft drink brands' goodwill valuation can increase. Then, Coca Coke may believe that there are many soft drinkers prefer to choose other soft drink brands' soft drinks to drink. So, global soft drink markets still have competitive effort. Coco Coke nees to learn how to change its taste and let soft drinkers believe its soft drink can bring health to them to compare other soft drink brands. So, it seems that goodwill valuation also helps any organizations to eveluate how market changes to influence itself product sale effort. It explains why goodwill valuation is one kind of good market changing predictable tool t any businesses in accpunting concept, instead of sale business valuation measurement tool.

On conclusion, accounting principle or accounintg concept is not only be applied to bookkeeping financial record aspect. If the organization hopes to find what factors to influence its customer number or they hope to predict whether market will ought how to change to be netter or worse. It may attempt to investigate its past every year some kinds of expenditure amount record in order to find how any why the firm itself needed to pay more or less to the kind of expenditure. It aims to research what factors may influence its past and present expenditur changes in order to find whether what the most influential factors are influenced itself buyers number increases or decreases . Hence, accounting is one kind of makret research scientific method to any organizations.

Accounting science how predicts e-commerce consumer behavior

Cash e-commerce organizations apply accounting record to predict consumer behaviors? If it is true, how e-commerce organizations can use past accounting record to predict consumer behaviors? In general, e-commerce sale transactions must need any individual e-buyers to register higher address to their e-store in order to deliver products to any one-buyer homes. For Amazon e-commerce organization, when one China client buys a furniture from US Amazon e-commerce organization, when one China client buys a furniture from US Amazon e-store. The furniture is putted to Amazon US itself warehouse. So, when the China e-buyer pays visa to buy the furniture . He needs to register his address to amazon e-store. When amazon confirms that it can receive cash from the China e-buyer visa card, then amazon will deliver the furniture from US amazon warehouse to the China e-buyer home by plane.

So, amazon must have any e-buyer address record and the product sale price record for any one country e-buyer after it comfirms that the e-buye visa card has enough money to buy the product. Thus, amazon can apply past every online transaction to follow these data to do market research, they may include: which country person buys the product, what the product is, how much to the product price, how many of different product number e-buyer purchase within the year. So, amazon can collect all above data to analyze any one country has the highest e-buyer number,e.g. in the year, there ar one million US e-buyers number, there are two million China e-buyer number,which kind of products are the most popular, e.g. soap , computer, furniture, cloth, shoe, shirt, towel, electronic products etc. what the age range is, e.g. young , old, students , workpeople, they choose to buy the kind of product, how many number , the family buys the kind of product to the e-transaction, how many goods return number to the year total e-transaction, how many goods return number to the year total e-transactions. Hence, amazon can gather all past every e-transaction data to prepare how to predict whether how every country e-transaction will consumer behavior to predict whether how every country e-transaction will influence consumer behavior will change next year in order to let it to prepare how to implement new market strategy,e.g. how to advertise its product, which countries need to spend more advertise to promote its products, evaluate whether amazon needs to spend how much advertisement expenditure to earn more e-sale transactions number to the targe sale country.

Why does amazon's any one e-transaction's accounting record assists it to predict consumer behavior? For china target e-buyers market example, when one Shanghai city e-buyer pays visa to buy one computer from amazon e-store, if the e-transaction can be accepted . Amazon can gather the e-buyer is living in China Shanghai city, which brand of computer , he chooses to buy, how much sale price to the computer, how many of computers number , he buys, how many e-transaction times to the China, Shanghai city buyer within the year. Hence, when amazon needs know where China target market has how many e-buyers number to every city, how many e-transaction return goods and refind number, which kinds of product are the popular to China e-buyers' purchase needs, which is the highest price and the lowest price sale level to China, Shanghai city target e-commerce market every e-transaction . Thus, when amazon collestc all above China, Shanghai past one year any individual e-transaction data, it can compare whether how its China, Shanghai city.

Nest year, e-buyers behavior change in order to analyze whether which kinds of product price ought need to reduce in order to attract many China e-buyers to click amazn webstores to pay visa to buy its products or which kinds of product price may increase, when the kind of product is popular to sell to China target market, or make out of e-stock shelf decision to the kind of product when Amazon discovers the kind of product is not accepted to buy in popular from its e-store. Thus, it seems that Amazon's past any one e-transaction accountning record can help it to analyze whether how every target market its e-buyer behavior is changing in order to change next year sale changing strategy is more reasonable . Hence, it explains why e-commerce organization's accounting record may help it to analyze how future market changes as well as record how every old e-buyer customer whether he/she will choose to buy the kind of old product again or buy new product, even not buy anything from Amazon e-stores this year.

Hence, any e-commerce organization's e-stores can apply online technology skil and accounting concept to help it to learn how to analyze every year post efficient countries' cities different e-buyer individual product behavioral choice in order to judge/revise whether it ought need to change to buy its products from its e-stores conveniently. So, any e-commerce organization explains why it can attempr to apply its post every accounting e-buyer sale transaction record to make every country consumer behavior marketing analysis to compare transaction visiting shop business model more easily, because visiting shop sale model can let the seller to sell its products in its shop, when it locates in the country. But e-commerce sale model can let the product can be sold to different countries more easily.

So, it seems that if the e-commerce organization can have good accounting record system to keep its past all e-transactions record can gather all data concerns any countries e-buyer individual address , how much sale price for the product, how many sold, and refund to the country e-buyers and the e-buyer age is young or old , male or female e-buyer purchase habit.

Can the e-commerce organizatin predict consumer behavior if it implemented inefficiency accounting record system? Firstly, we need to know good or right accounting record system can help the organization to track or find past any transactions more easily. So, if the organization has none good accounting record system , its accounting record system can not be improved efficiently. Then, its accounting record may bring wrong sale price record, wrong profit (over -profit) or less profit or wrong loss (over loss) number record. Then, this wrong sale transaction record may mislead financial performance to publis to know, e.g. current year, its sale performance is improved, but in fact, its current year sale number is less than last year sale number. Consequently, this organization can not predict its consumer behavior. Whether know to change exactly, due to it often has wrong sale number record, e.g. higher or lesser sale price record, and more or less sale number may influence its gross profit earns high amount, even if its any kinds of expense record is more orless, it will influence its net profit is more or less or less is more or less, for example, if the organization earns US one million dollar prodict this year, but due to it smore sale number transaction to cause over profit. So, its financial performance report indicated its earned US two million dollar. So, it believes its buyers number can increase, if its sale prices do not change. This wrong financial performance report many mislead it has good consumer behavior in this year. Then, it will continue implement its old marketing strategy. Consequently, its next year financial performance may be caused worse to compare present. So, it implies that wrong financial record may cause wrong consumer behavior judgement.

Can robots perform management accounting analysis tasks
Our future will experience artificial intelligent

development stage. Nowadays, we had had some tasks which can be done by robots, e.g. warehouse delivery, restaurnt kitechen dish cleaning tasks, transport tasks, even non drive manual auto driving tasks, shopping center service etc. cleaning or customer service simple jobs duties. If one day, robots cab be applied to do office tasks, e.g. accounting record tasks, they may replace account clersk, even accountants to deal simple accounting record tasks, even complicate management account analysis tasks in office working environment. If future robots can be developed to help accounts clerks as well as accountants to do simple bookkeeping debit and credit every income ot expense transaction record in order to analyze marketing research tasks, then it brings this question: Can future robots replace accounts clerks and accountants to do their accounting tasks in any organizations. I shall attempt to research the relationship between robots and accounting tasks questions as well as whether robots will bring what social influence if robots can replace future human to do any simple and complex accounting tasks for any organizations.

What is need for development of artificial intelligence to accounting tasks aspect? The first computer language used to create artificial intelligence is USP. This language is quite flexible and extensive . Features such rapid prototyping and macro are very useful in creating AI. LISP is a language that makes complex tasks simple. So it seems that it is possible tobots can learn human to do any kinds of accounting tasks, e.g. financial account record, audit check, management account analysis etc. different kinds of acounting tasks for financial , management account, audit check functions in any organizations.

However, scientists believe that artificial intelligence can help accountants be more productive and efficient. Robotic process automation RPA) allows machines or AI workers to complete repetitive, time-consuming tasks in business processed, such as document analysis, handling that are plentiful in accounting . AI can also significantly reduce financial fraud and maintenance accounting errors. Hence, the stages of AI development to accoutning industry, they may include: internet AI, business AI, perception AI, and autonomous AI ., Internet AI is thr simplest stage of AI, business AI has a limted memory, perception AI. This is the first stage in the future of AI. A key feature of this perceptive form of AI is the ability to compile and draw from past experiences, much like human to accounting tasks.

The design phase is essentially in literative process comprising all the steps releveant to building the AI or machine learning model, data acquisition, exploration, management and analsis tasks. So, it seems that future robots may be developed to help human to do simple and complex accounting tasks. Combining AI with other technologies, such as robotic, process automation can follow accountants to redirect the time that they used to spend on multiple tasks, toward performing high-value, high -impact taaks. Adding AI to accounting operation can also increase output quality by miniizing human errors. So, AI and automation won't be replacing finance and accounting professionals in the foreseeable futue.

On the contrary, as AI automates many aspects of business, there is a bug opportunity for accounting and finance professsionals to upskill themselves to meet the requirements of the 21 centurey. For AI audit task aspect, AI enables the analysis of a full populatin of data and can identify outliers or expectations. By making it possible for auditors to work better and smarter. AI will help them to optimize their time, enabling them to use their human judgement to analyze a boarder and deeper set of data and documents.

Can AI be used in auditing and accounting ? In the assurance practice, AI is being used to perform auditing and accounting prcedures, such as review of general ledgers, tax compiance, preparing workpapers, data analytic, expense compliance, fraud accounting skills. So, it seems that future AI can replace market research analysists, compensation and benefits managers , instead of financial accountants, management accountants an auditors in any organizations.For bookkeeping clerks position example, these simple account jobs are expected to decrease, by 8% 2024, and it's non surprise because most bookkeeping is getting automated if it has not been as of now, Quickbook, Peachtrss etc. accounting software that does not need any more, because robots do not need any kinds of accounting software to help them to do any simple or complex accounting tasks.

How has teachnology changed the accounting industry? Computers and accounting softeare has changed the industry complexity, with but when robots develop, it will change global accountancy professional more complex. Can robots replace accountants? Automation had brought significant changes the accounting profession over the last decaed. When some tools have made accountants lives easier. However, since robots invention, it developed these tools have also created a false debate about whether automation will overtake the global accounting industry compexity and make accountants irrelvant . The question should not be whether automation will take over accounting, but where its rreal value lives.

In fact, I believe that no any software can match the critical thinkning and trusted counsel that a human advisor offes, as valued accountants, have become business partners, where software is limited to evaluating concrete inputs, accountants can understand clients business goals and observations voice to make decisions. This allows them to serve as advisors to their clients, whether by adjusting business models in real time, or managing emplyer wellbeing . Sok, future AI development ought not replace human accountant's this kind of skill more easily.

● How robotic process automation impact on accouting industry changes?

Searching for methods to efficiently perform accounting tasks can be dated book to the 1950 s, when process mechanisation involved the use of punched cards to store and retrieve transaction data (Keenoy, 1958). Since then IT ad automation have transtormed the way accountants collect, store, process and share data through a variety of tools (Ellis, 1986); Kaye, Nicholson, 1992; Rom, Rohde, 2007). However, robotis process automation is a technology solution that allows end-users to comfigure a software robot to use existing applications to perform accounting transactions manipulate data and communcation with other systems (introduction to robotis, 2015).

Software robots can be easily programmed or trained to perform repetitive, rules-based , high volume operations by replicating human actions when accessing multiple systems, applications, and documents (Embracing robotic automation 2018). Hence, robotic accounting software can bring cost reduction to counting and finance tasks, e.g. one robotic accounting software can replace two to five full time accounting clerks, increased process speed, software robots perform routime tasks faster than employees would manage mamually (Cacity, Willcocks, 2016) . They do not get distracted or tried and thus avoid delays, cycle times decreases significantly improved process control and performance visibility, e.g the collected analytical information is much more detailed and can be used for audit and compliance checks, higher quality data (accuracy, consistency, compliance), e.g. robots can validate the data before reporting or using them future. Assuming that the appropriate rules have been thoroughly tested beforehand, data inaccuracy and quality risk decrease fill tracking and logging robots' action make internal and external audits easier and reduce compliance risks, continuous operation 24 hours a day, or none working day limits. So, robots are applied on accounting task aspect, it can bring positive impact on employees, repetive tasks taken over by robots release employees' times. They can shift their focus on higher value added tasks, solve employee morale proble,. Any accounting department staffs may feel tired when they need over time works, often but robotic accounting staff won't have tired or bored feeling.

However, robotic process, automatin may be applied on these accounting tasks aspect, they may include: internal control period end clising, general ledger, subledgers, closing , validatin of journal entries, low-risk accounts, reconsiliation, consolidation, reporting-monthly , quarterly close, internal performance and management reportng aggregating and analysing financial and operational data, external statutary report, accounts receivable and payable record-maintaining updating customer/supplier data, creating processing, posting payment, collections, billing, matching invoices, aganist sales and purchase orders, cash management, general accoutning, inter-company transactions, inventory accountancye, travel and expenses reimbursement request, audit and document expense report, payroll, stock keeping, fixed asset accouting record, tax accounting. So, the general simple accounting tasks robots will have effort to finish.

● Can robots perform the same management accounting analytical decision making skills to human management accountants tasks?

Although, robots can perform simple bookkeeping audit accounting tasks, but whether complex management accounting analytical and decision making tasks, robots can do the same level of management accounting analytical, decision making tasks to human management accountants?

I shall attempt to answer this question. How robots impact of mental accounting in valuation? No retailers show this price without considering the " 99" in end. This indicates to our mind that the price is cheaper. Its popularity can be verified gas stations all around the world. The difference between robots mental accounting issue and management accountants.

The Anchoring theory was used to verify its possible impacts on capital venture tech finds decisions, during equity trading for an initial investment starting. Management accountants ususally arrange 68% of the finds use-valuation as a basic, when 21% proposed other methods . But still use valuation and only 11% of the investors said they did not consider valuation at allo. the context considered that the human management accountant will consider that the investment would be made in a startup in early stages. That is with little or any real accounting information can image the amount of uncertainty that exists in the type of analysis?

Moreover, why do even experienced fund managers invest based on an impossible calculation> In simplity, it explains that human management accountant in order to do any investment decision. Although robotis will use alaytic mind more than calculating to estimate any investment risk in order to make investment decsion for any organizations. AI's analytic skill and human management accountant calculation risk skill be their difference on how dealing management accounting investment risk issue aspect. Even, the difference between human management accountant and robotic management accounting automation is their robotic management automation can apply mental accounting theory to judge consumer behavioral choice.

It is a new model of consumer behavior is developed using a hyrod of psychology and microeconomics. The deveopment of the model starts with the mental coding of combinations of risks and losses using the prospect theory value finction. Then, robotic management accounting automatin can attempt to evaluate of consumer purchase for the product is modeled using the new concept of " transaction utility", e.g. one family electronic firm, it is seeling rice cooker, television radio, household electronic products, it can learn how to mental accounting method to help this houseold electronic product firm to predict how any why its different kinds of household electronic products choice may change to its consumer behavior next week, e.g. robots can gather wlectronic product competitors prices data to compare itself company's same kinds of electronic product data e.g. rice cooker prices and its competitors' rice cookers prices, whether its high price , rice cookers price factor or other factors influence its rice cookers sale number decreases in this week. Consequently robotic management accounting software may help this household elecronic product company to analyze whether what are the actual factors to influence its rice cookers prces reduce in this week. It is human management accountants feel difficult to collect past price data in order to make accurate consumer behavior changes, prediction or find whther are the main factors to influence product sale number increases or decreases.

Hence, future robotic management accounting automation can learn the valuation of purchase modeled using the new concept of transactin utulitym such as this houseold electronic product case, robotic management accounting automation many learn the household budget process ,the characterization of mental accounting, in order to find whether household purchase behavior to the company's products whether what the main factors may influence its household producys sale number increases or decreased.

On conclusion, future robots can do simple bookkeeping, audit check , general daily accounting tasks, even robots can also do complex management accounting tasks, they can learn how to apply mental accounting knowledge to gather the company's past all every month different price variable data, sale number, in order to conclude whether what are the main factors to influence the kind of product sale number increases or decreased more accurately to compare human management accountants in any organizations.

Applying HR management accounting learns consumer behavior

Managerial accounting purposes to be used by management in "making by business decision: It includes product caost, budget , forecast and various financial analysis consumer behavior is the series of behaving of patterns that consumers follow before making a purchase through consumer behavior, you can also earn how customers interact with and the year products. So, any organizations may attempt to find any management account past year past per month transaction records to bring consumer behavioral change predictiver knowledge, it can help future decisions about product creation more easily.

Hence , the management accoutning knowledge focuses the process of creating organization goals by identifying, measuring, analyzing, interpreting and communicating informations to managers is call management or manerical accounting. Management accounting focuses on all accounting aimed at informing management about operational business metics. Also, any managers may attempt to gather past product number presentation date to find whether what the main factors can influence consumer buying behavioral change in its any kinds of products, the level of motivation also affects the buying behavior of customers, e.g. whether the products' sale prices sight rise, to influence customer number reduces, or whether the product's traditional old design is not more attractive or popular to accept to compare other linds of competitors' similar product design, or whether the kind of product is not popular to be accpeted to use, the another how invention of similar product ot the market is recession , it need to change another new sale market, if replaces its existence etc. different factors.

Hence, management accounting can help managers to attempt to gather past the product's sale and production past data to carry on analyzing whether what the main factor to influence its customer number reduces or increases in other to improve its sale strategy.

● Computer sale applies management accounting to predict consumer behavior

For computer sale product example, the computer saller may attempt to apply management accounting to analyze why computer buyer behavioral changes, e.g. a study of consumer behavior will reveal what kind of consumers buy computers, could they buy for home and personal use or for office, what features , they look for, what benefit o they seek including post purchase service, huw much they are willing to pay how many they are likely to buy . All of these computer buyer individual purchase behavioral analysis, the computer seller can follow its different models of laptops, desttops, prices, sale number, house or office ise design kind etc. data to research and analyze and predict hether future computer buyer individual need will how changes, in order to prepare and learn how to design new kinds of desktops and laptops to raise competitve effort.

In fact, in computer industry, the factors may influence computer buyer behavioral change, they may include core technical features, past purchase services, price and payment, conditions, physical appearanre, value added features and connectivity and ability are the main seven factors that are influencing consumers' laptop purchases choices.

● How can the laptop computer seller applies management accounting data to analyze whether which is the main factor to influence laptop buyer behavior changes?

for last month, I assume that laptop model (A) laptop computer sale price si per US$1000 and it can sold 1000 number and laptop model (B) laptop computer sale price is per US$1,500 and it can sold 2000 number.SO, it implies that although laptop model (B) computer sale price is more than US$500 to compare laptop model (A) computer, but the model (B) laptop computer can still sell more than 1000 number fo compare model (A) laptop computer last moth. It seems that model (B) laptop's attractive dsign, more fuction, rapid connectivity and mobility and attrative physical appearance main factors may influence laptop (B) model computer products sale number is more than laptop (A) model computer products last month. But, in this month, it has significant change between laptop model (A) and laptop (B). In this month, laptop modle (A) and laptop model (B) prices are not changes, but laptop model (A) can sell 3,000 number and laptop model (B) can sell only 500 number. Consequently, their sale numbers have significantly changes, laptop (A) can increase more 2,000 sale number, but laptop model (B) can decrease 1,500 sale number between these two months. It explains that although it seems that laptop (B) model has possible own attractive physical appearance, and rapid connectivity and mobility, more function to cause it can sell more than laptop (A) model computer produc. But, it ensures that all of anh one these possible factors can not help it to raise sale number in long time. It means that laptop model (B) may have other factors to influence itss sale number, e.g. other brand of laptop computers' physical appearance, more function, connectivity and mobility , features , even they can provide better value added sale service, repair service, product delivery service, feature to compare this brand of laptop seller, or its laptop model (B) buyers had lost confidence to use its laptop model () computer products, because they often need to repair and pay extra repair service fee frequently, e.g. one year has one time to two times at least per year. SO, their past poor frequent repair experience influences they choose to buy other brand of laptops. Otherwise, why laptop model (A) computer products number can sell more 2,000 number , the factor may include non rising price, none frequent past repair experiences to any one model (A) laptop buyer , their individual psychological positive feeling factor . So, it seems that gather these two laptop model (A) and model (B) past sale number, sale price data to conclude whther what main factors may influence its model (A) and model (B) laptop sale number to increase or decrease in long term.

However, this laptop computer seller can not only depend on the gathering these two months short time sale numbers ans sale prices data to model (A) and (B) laptops, in order to make the final conclusion concerns whether what the main factor can influence model (A) and model (B) laptop product sale number changes absolutely. It must need to continue to keep the long time management sale umber and sale prie data record for laptop (A) and (B) in order to conclude whether what the most accurate influential factor is that it can influence laptop model (A) and B() sale number both change in order to implement the improvement strategy for them both.

● Management accounting data can also help this laptop seller to predict future market development or whether which market will have high sale effort, e.g. Japan laptop sale market may have the highest market share ratio, among different Asia countries, or Germany laptop sale market may have highest market share ratio among different European countries next year. For example, in the last year, this laptop computer seller had sold 50,000 laptops to Japan computer market, it has sold 500,000 laptops to China computer market, it has sold 100,000 laptops to US computer market and 50,000 laptops to Germany computer market, in this year. its these laptop markets sale prices are not changed, it has sold 200,000 laptops to japan computer market, it has sold 400,000 laptops to China computer market, it had sold 200,000 laptops to US computer market and 200,000 laptops to Germany computer market . Hence, it ensures that Germany laptop market has increased 4 times sale number from last year and Japan has increased 4 times sale number from last year. Otherwisem China laptop sale number has decreased 100,000 laptops from last year and US laptop sale number has increased 1 time from last year. So, it can imply that Germany and Japan future laptop sale number may grown rapidly to compare US and CHina laptop sale markets. It also indicates this sale trend also may help this laptop computer to attempt to find whether what factors may influence its US and China laptop sale number fells down,e.g. whether this local laptop choices increasing factor, it laptop physical appearance is not more attraction, or slow connectivity and mobility speed ,even their model (A) and () laptop prices are higher to compare US and China local other similar brands of laptops prices.

In summary, I believe that management accounting technique can be attempted to apply to help any kinds of products to find whether what main factor(S) to influence their product sale number changes, it is one kind of good data gathering and analytical tool to help any businesses to attempt to predict consumer behavioral changes.

Organization management accounting strategy
What is organization management accounting strategy? As its most basic an organization management accounting

strategy is a plan that specifies how your business will allocate resources, e.g. money, labour, and inventory to suppoty production, marketing, inventory and other business activities. IN general, the foure organizational straategy and the culture of the organization categorized into four types: Adhocracy, market and hierarchy.

The purpose of an organization management accounting strategy can be defined as the direction an organization takes with the aim of achieving future business success. Strategy sets out how an organization intends to employ its resources, including the skills and knowledge of its people as well as financial and material assets, in order to achieve its mission or overall targets. So, the key element of an organizational strategy may include: define vision, create mission, set objectives, develop strategy, outline approach, get down to tactics. However, an organizatinal strategy plan is an organizational management activity that is used to set priorities, focus energy and resources, strengthen operations, ensure that employees and other stakeholders are working toward common goals established agreement crowd intended outcomes/ results, and access organizational missions.

Adhocracy strategy is a form of business management accounting that emphasizes individual initiative and self organization in order to accomplish tasks. This is in contrast to bureaucracy which relies on a set of defined rules and set hierarchy in accomplishing organizational goals. The term was popularized by Alvin Toffler in the 1970s. Examples of adhocracy include most project or marix organizations. Among private-sector organizations, high technology firms, particularly young firms facing fierce competition are sometimes organized as adhocracies. However, important examples of adhocracy do exist in government. Hence, adhocracy is a flexible, adoptable and informal form of organization that is defined by a lack of formal structure that employs specialized multidisciplinary trams grouped by functions. Adhocracy is characterized by an adoptive , creative and flexible behavior based on non-performance. Adhocray culture in a business context, is a corpoate culture based on the ability to adapt quickly to changing conditions. Adhocracies ar characterized by flexibility, employee empowerment and an emphasis on individual initiative.

The five basic marketing strategies may include: product, price and promotion and people in management accounting strategy aspect. They are key marketing elements used to position a business strategically. A market strategy refers to a business's overall game plan for reaching prospective consumers and turning them into customers of their products and services. For example, the BSC business 2 customed marketing strategies may include : social networks and viral marekting, paid media advertising, internet marketing, email marketing, direct selling, point-of-purchase marketing, co-branding, cause marketing, conversational marketing. Hence, marketing strategy or management accounting strategy is a long term toeard looing approach and an overall game plan of any organization or any business with the foundemental goal of achieving a competitive advantage by understanding the needs and wants of customers.

Hierarchy strategy describes a relations of corporate strategy and sub-strategies hierarchically and logically consistent at the level of vision, mission, goals, and metrics , e.g. HR strategy (human resource strategy), to general, the three levels of strategy are: corporate level strategy, this level answers the foundamental question of what you want to achieve, business unit level strategy focuses on how you've going to grow.

The management accounting strategy planning hierarchy is the organization's mission and vision both of ,which should be long-lasting and motivating. At the base of the hierarchy are the shorter term strategies and tactics that unit members will use to achieve the vision. So, the basic levels of management accounting strategy are: corporate, business, functional and operational level strategy. The strategic hierarchy aims to be concept used to understand the different types of strategy decision made in a organization, e.g. michael porter , three generic strategies (cost leadership, differentation, and focus) that can be implemnted at any organizations. So, hierarchical levels of strategy managment accounting may be concerned with selection of which is the right generic strategy to implement, sale method, such as low product sale price, lot differentiation of product choice, and focus an main product feature market sale methods etc.

● The relationship between organizational management accounting strategy and avoiding resource waste

If an organization can implement good managment accounting strategy whether it can assist it to reduce any organizational internal resource waste, e.g. exceed human resource employment cost, facility used cost, using cost, efficient administration or management cost etc. essential organizational cost. Because any organizations must need to use resources in order to achieve efficient providivities, service activities, if the organization can implement effective strategy in order to measure its performance, whether strategy can assist it to judge how to avoid not essential resources spending. Can efficient strategy help organizations to avoid to waste resources? I shall attempt to explain as below:

Whether formal strategy implement can avoid formal technical measurement of scale and concentrates on the loca resource mobilization using aspect os small, medium and large organization? What does resource mobilization strategy mean? Resource mobilization refers to all activities involved in sesuring new and additional resources for your organization. It also involves making better use of and maximizing , existing resources.What are the stepd in resource mobilization?

Firstly, any organizations need to plan od designing a resource moilization strategy and action plan, secondary , finding key elements of a resource mobilization strategy, thirdly,act of practical step to implementatin, fourth identify, fifth step, engagement, sixth step, negotiate, eventh step, manage and report, final step, communicating results. What are the source of resource mobilization to any organizations? For example includes spreading flyers, holding community meetings, and recruiting volunteers. Material may include financial and physical capital, like office space, money, equipment, and supplies . Human resources, such as labour experience, skills and expertise in a certain field.

How does an entrepreneur mobilize resources? To exploit opportunities, entrepreneurs monilize and recombine a variety of resources, such as financial capital (e.g. cash, ot loan from a bank , human capital e.g. skills from a employees, and social capital e.g. information obtained from social contracts. Hence, the overall objectives of the resource mobilization strategy is to secure the necessary funds to deliver on the source mobilization strategic outcomes. To achieve this accurate resource used number and expenditure budget and emergency appeals will need sufficient preditable and contrributions. So, the aim of resource mobilization strategy outlines how secretariat will organize the process of prioritising, plannin, selecting projects, monitoring: broadening the resource channels, as well as coordinating with staffs for mobilising and effectively utilizing resources.

So, the genesis of resource mobilization strategy is a good, solid strategic plan, it should articulate activities that are more routine in nature and can be finded through the organizational internal efficient resource mobilization. Resource mobilization refers to all activities involves in securing . These new directions or new business opportunities are pursued using a distinct resource mobilization strategy .

On conclusion , an efficient resource mobilization plan is a term resource mobilization, it refers to all activities undertaken by an organizations to secure new and additional financial, human and material resources to advance its mission. Inherent in efforts to mobilize resources is the drive for organizational sustainability . So, resource mobilization is about an organization getting the resources that are needed to be able to do the work it has planned. Resource mobilization is more that just fundraising, it is about getting a range or resources from a wide range of resource providers for donors, through a number of different mechanisms. How does an entrepreneur mobile resources? To exploit opportunities, entreprensurs mobilize and combine a variety of resources, such as financial captial , e.g. cash or loans from a bank, human capital e.g. skill from an employee and social capital e.g. information obtained from social contract.

Why do organizations need resource mobilization strategy?

The reasons may include: The principles of resource mobilization wih examples, it focuses on forging partnerships built on trust and mutual accountability . So, as to attract adequate and more predictable contributions, with the future goal of sustainability, it refers to all undertaken by an organizatin to secure new and additional financial , human and material resource to advance its mission, in efforts to mobilize resources is the drive for organizational sustainability, community mobilization is the process of bring together as many stakeholders as possible to raise people's awareness of and demand for a particular programme to assist in the delivery of resources and services, and to strengthen community participation for sustainability an dself -reliance, resource mobilization is often referrred t as " new business creaating chance" , the organization has a strong, yet flexible structure , such as writing proposal how to spend the least respurce expenditure in order to achieve the most satisfactory effective result to the organization.

Hence, developing a resource mobilization strategy plan , as the source of new business opportunities to the social and behavioral change considerations must be needed the organization as well as resource mobilization target at a minimum level should be needed to raise at transformational change happen on the ground and advocate for the products and may have to develop new business proposal.

● Can resource mobilization change improve organizational performance?

I believe that resource mobilization can help any organizations to change or improve performance to the better, even the best. I shall explain as below:

What are the sources of organizational change? Change originates in either the external or internal environments of the organization. External sources include political, social, technological or economic environment, externally motivated change may involve government action, technology development, competition , social values and economic variables.

How do organizational resources affect change? Results indicate that organizations possessing greater stocks of historically valuable resources were much less likely to engage in adaptive strategic change, but also that this resoure-driven towards change tended to have a even beneficial effect on performance . Wonder of organizational change management is easier spoken about than achieved by resource mobilization strategic in possible? Can create enterprise level value by effective process for resource allocation?

The key to success involves managing organizational change , so it leads to real and lasting improvements, tailoring to resource allocation how mobilization strategy. So, nowadays, organizational capacty for change: Increasing change capacity and avoiding change overload, organization, today risk is overcommitting resources, resulting in an overload condition wih which it how allocates its resources to tbe used efficiently or inefficiently. For example, on new government regulations, ne products development or growth aspect, organizational change efforts often run into some form of human resistance. First, management staffed its human resource departments with spend most of that time in efficiency. So, whether how organizational change is better, it depends on how it changes its old resources, e.g. human resource, facility, equipment resources, even management time resources to change new improvement resources change to be better . It means providing the resources, budget, authority, credibility and commitment for the effort to truly organizational change on improvement.

● Why does organizational resource budget need?

For example, managing a human resource department involves budget planning and execution . The human resources budger refers to the finds that how HR allocates to all HR processes. Unit should include in an HR budget. It may include: number of employees, projected for next year, benefits cost increases or decreases, salary cost increases or decreases, projected turnover rate, calculation, actual cost incured in the current year, new employee welfare benefits. programs planned, other changes in policy, business strategy , it may impact costs on HR cost aspect. So, an organization needs to budget whether it will have how much on what kinds of resources spending aspect, including human resources, facility, equipment and water , electricity etc. natural resource , it budget is a tool used for planning and controlling financial resources. It is a guideline for future plan of action, espressed in financial terms within a set of period time, knowing organization's priorities, objectives and goals helps it prepare organization resource budget.

Effectively leveraging people and budget, resource management is critical for organizations to ensure . They are optimizing and allocating resources to the right initiations, e.g. from a human resource perspective, the data needed to create a new budget include the following number of employees, working arrangement tasks time, management time, employee salary cost, due to costs that only impact the human resource department and impacts the entire organization both aspects. So, efficient HR cost budget can help refine goals that reflect realistic resources and how memebers of the organization to use fund because employee retirement can be expensive and it can b increased or decreased expense in any time, when the month needs increase or decrease employees number to any departments. It depends on whether tasks rate is needed to increase or decrease. So, an organization's HR cost budget can help how it makes the most accurate HR resource expenditure.

Organizational facility, equipment, shop, office, warehouse space resource budget why is important. Office space is as an enabling resource, equipment and furniture to enhance the organization's ability to achieve efficient operations and activities of the best organizational performance. In view of this analysis, facility planning personal would be one important factor to influence whether the organizatin can spend the least expenditure to use its resource. During business growth, any facility equipment, office , shop, warehouse space must increase , moreover staff puts increasing number on existing resources, so be sure to budget in order to make another option is to least equipment instead of buying it, whether you need moving insurance for important equipment and machinery, set budget to help prevent overspending.

All of the tasks that are include in maintaining a facility, such as equipment maintenance and building facilities whether are needed to improve, facility oversight, warehouse and special equipment whether is qpproriate space for customer service and uses resource dynamic of an organization's work patterns with work. It depends partly on the resources an organization is willing to invest or not, when it feels this facility resources are very important to influence its performance.

● What does organization office , shop , warehouse space resource management strategy?

Organization and using space must be land resource, if the organization can manage how to use its space in efficiency, then it can improve service performance or productive efficiency. Space management can be defined as a practice where an organization manages its physical space invnetory which includes tracking , control, supervision and utilization, planning of the space available. So, space management is the mangement of an organization's physical space inventory. Ths involves the tracking of how much space an organization has managing occupancy information and creating spatial plans. So, one efficient space resource using organization, it needs to undertake annual property assessment reviews, leverage individual projects to drive portfolio evoluation applya planning methodology on all project rises, utilize planning to define direction and scope focus on mathematics before graphics, define and collect only the required data on warehouse, shops, office, buildind space using aspect. For example, a space management ffice can give the organizatin an accurate picture of how many employees , it needs to have space for an average day, and show it the trends of demand for this space across weeks and months. This can help the organization to determine how many permanent desks could be converted to hot desks in office, warehouse or shop , saving space. For example, space managementin retail aspect, it is the process of managing the floor space adequately to facilitate the customers and to increase the sale.

Shop space management is very crucial in retail as the sales volume and gross profitability depends on the amount of space used to generate those sales. Space management is a multi-step process that requires data gathering, analysis , forecast and strategizing. In prective, it involes creating a space management system that occupants throughout your organization, so whether the organization realizes it or not, every organization needs to know how to manage its space one way or another , if it hopes to improve its service or productive performance. Make use of these strategic space management and planning techniques, efficient and an unplanned, unmanaged office is not likely to magically transofrm into a well organized of productivity. So, space management is the management of an organization's physical space inventoty , employee working environment, shop product putting sheleves locatin, equipment, desk putting location. All of this tangible space physical factor may influence overall organizational service and/or productive performance and /or sale performance. So, space may be an organization's land usng resource because any organization's land using space must be limited size, they must have land space using shortage challenge if their products stock number increases, but warehouse space can not increase or shop products shelves number can not increase, but product sale number increases.

● The relationship netween organization behavior and resource using management accounting

Has organizational behavior and resource spending, they have close cause and effect direct relationship ? When one organization can perform better, whether it represents that it must spend much resource to use or when it perform poor, it represents that it must not spend much resource to use. Organizational behavior is a field of study that investigates the impact that organizational psychology and human resource management, the cause and effect relationship.

How organizational behavior effects an oganization? Organizational behaviors propose that inventives are motivational factors that are crucial for employees to perform well. It changes the way people make decisions, e.g. decision to increase or decrease resources to use, when the organization feels that it has resource shortage or excess. However, businesse that are able to encourage risks in decision making within the company culture can enhance innovation and creativity.

In fact, organizational behavior has four main elements, people, structure, technology and external environment. So , tangible and intangable resources may influence organization behavior when it is needed to change by management, e.g. human behavior in a work environmen and determines its impacts on job structure, performance, communication, motivation, leadership etc. for example, when the manager has less time to prepare how to organize this meeting process to his client. His short managing meeting plan time , intangible time resource, it can influence his business proposal to be either accepted or rejected to this client. So , time resource whether it is enough or not. It can influence this manager's client proposal meeting whether it is accepted or rejected in possible.

Every employee behavior can determine the importance of group departments in business productivity. So, it seems that resources whether they are enough , they can impact on employee's performance. As a result, managers are able to maintain better relation with their employees by effective utilization of human resource. So, cause and effect relationship plays an important rolw in how an individual is likely to behave in a enough tangible and intangible resource provided or not enough organization.

Modern organizational behavior is characterised by the acceptance of a human resource model, e.g. whether the plant can provide enough productive equipment facility and space shelf for product putting location in order to raise or improve logistic transport efficiency in warehouse. So, plant warehouse space management and shelf putting location productive equipment facility these tangible resource factors may influence warehouse productive performance. It seems that tangible resource provision amount and space management or intangible resource time management resource, they have close relationship to influence organizational behavior. Consequently, it can achieve the result either performance improvement or worse performance. So, resource and performance organizations , they ought have cause and effect relationship in resource management mobilization strategy view.

● How applying artificial intelligent management accounting solution accounting challenges

One of the biggest challenges for management accountants nowadays is the preparation to face globalization in local and global market. Globalization competition is changing government regulation and innovation in technology had to change in the market environment which have greater impact to an organization. The role of managemet accounting to AI, it may help managers to make any management strategy decision, e.g. evaluate sale price is the most reasonable, sale market choice, customer age target evaluation etc. within any organizations. Also known of cost accunting, management account of the process of identifying, analyzing and communicating information to managers to help to achieve business goals. However, the most important job of management accountant is t condoct a relevant cost analysis to determine the existing expenses and give suggestion for the future activities and make better management accounting, when management accountants need to learn how to apply these management accounting data: financial planning, financial statement analysis, cost accounting, find flow and cash flow analysis, standard , marginal cost and budgetary control, they can be made by AI.

In general, the job dutures of management accountant may include: generate sale among client accounts, operates as the point of contact for assigned customers, develops and maintains long term relationships with accounts, makes sure clients receives requested produsts ans services in a timely fashion . So, they need to learn these different management accounting technique: margin analys, capital budget, inventory valuation and product cost, tend analysis and forecasting. Future AI may be taught to learn all of these any one management accounting technique to assist organizations to make more reasonable management account strategy implementation.

The basic principles of management accounting include communication presents insight which is crucial , irrelevance information is valuable, the influence one value is estimated, credibility,recognizing the requirement, good accounting manager, they need to learn how conflict, be open to new ideas: In management accounting tehnology apply, there are three elements of management control system to develop to future Artificial intelligent management accounting technology delegated decison authority , performance evaluation and measurement systems and compensation, reward system.

Hence, accounting technology in AI development has always played a past in making the accountant's job just a played a part in making the accountant's job just a easier. Its own knowledge of technology increased to have the accountant's ability to analyze statistical values. Technology advancements have enhanced the accountant's ability to interpret data efficiently and effectively.

● Future AI management accountant may help human to the honest accounting record

However, any one managment accountant needs have good professional personal quality, honestly and integrity play vital roles in accounting because they allow investors to trust the information they receive about companies in which they invest. Honesty in accounting is the primary characteristics of the profession that allows financial decision-makers to make appropriate judgement . So, the main focus of management accounting is to assist the management of a company in efficiency performing its function-planning, organizaing, divesting and controlling . Management accounting helps with these functions in the following ways: provides data, it serves to a vital source of data for planning, for product costing method example, it is used to cost methods available are process costing, job and different production and decision making. for 3 types of controls may include: internal controls are typically procedures or technical safe guards that are implemented to prevent problems and protect organizations' assets. Future AI technology may help an organizations to do above all management accounting decision jobs ,even replace human in offices to avoid losses. The traditional management accounting technique includes" the use of performance measures, three ROI , budget systems for planning and control, divisional profit reports and cost-profit volume relationship, and breakeven analysis for decisions. The management accounting reports may include order information report, project report, competitor analysis. They are either internally aor outsourced. All of these management accounting methods, future AI can replace human accountants to do .

● Can AI be applied to help organizations to implement management account strategies ?

The two widely used types of accounting are: Financial and management accoutning, for the strategic cost management techniques example, it is the cost management techniques that aims at reducing cost , when strengthening the position of the business. It is a process of combining the decision making structure with the cost information in order to do the strategy as a whole . Hence the role of management account in the organization is to support competitive decision making by collecting, processing and communicating information that helps management plan, control and evaluating business processes and company strategy . So, the strategy management accounting can be defined as the process of identifying, collecting , selecting and analyzing accounting data . So, future AI can be applied to assist accounting teams in strategic decision making and organization effectiveness assessment must be defined.

Future AI can be applied to these management accounting aspect: For methods and techniques of costing management , it may include: Job costing, advestment, salepeople,bonus, contract cost, long periods of time job, batch cost, process cost, one operation (unit or output) , cost service or operating costing, farm cost, multiple cooperation unit. The tools of cost analysis, breakeven analysis, budget cost control marginal cost analysis, cost control , minimum price analysis, standard cost development , target cost. All of these management strategies, AI can do .

The various tools and technique of marginal costing may include: contribution, profit volume ratio, contribution : sale value , p/v ratio, features of profit volume , break even point . Hence, the AI tools can control cost monitoring in execution. For that AI can help organizations to make cost control budget, it is defined as a AI tool that is used by the management of an organization in regulating and controlling of a manufacturing organization. AI can also perform cost budget for material to any manufacturing organizations to help them to reduce the manufacturing cost , e.g. making material choice for the cheapest price.

AI can gather the product material price, e.g. standard cost and normal cost. Then , AI can help the manufacturing organization to choose the best quality of the cheapest material in order to compare whether which kinds of material to produce the kind of product can bring the high economic benefit to let consumers get more satisfactory feeling. Thus, it is future management accounting development direction for AI.

IV

How social change influence market resource supply

The relationship between resource shortage and consumer behavior

Can resource shortage influence consumer behavior changes?

Can bring either positive or negative or both impact to change consumer behavior when the consumer begins to feel resource shrtage occurrence to choose to buy the kind of product or consume the kind of service?

Consumer researchers have suggedsted that chronic resource scaraity, specially, an inproveished early home environment with fewer resources and high levels of instability and uncertainty can lead to chronic differences in choice behavior (Griskevicius et al. 2011). How are consumers affected by scarcity? Scarcity affects producers because they have to make a choice on how to best ise their limited resources. It also affects consumers because they have to make a choice on what services or goods to chooce. Hence, resource shortage may be situational factor influence, situational influences are external circumstances or conditions existing when a consumer makes a purchase decision. Because the kind of product is facing resource shortage issue to influence the product manufacturer can not have enough resource to manufacture the kind og product. SO, number supply is decreasing, such as cars product, if steel number supply is decreasing, it can influence global car manufacture number decreases. When global new car buyers feel that they can not buy any kinds fo new cars easily. Then, even global new car price rises, they won't influence new car buyers purchase desires. So, in new car sale market, if steel supply number reduces, global new car buyer number will not decrease easily.

How does a consumer make choice with scarce resources? Like producers, consumers also have to make choices, since consumer resources , such as time, attention, and money are limited. They must choose how to best allocate them by making tradeoff. The concept of trade-offs due to scarcity is formalized by concept of opportunity cost. In fact, research in marketing often begins with two assumptions, by scarcity of products and/or a scarcity of resources, dfferent types of scarcity individually and jointly influence.

Consumer behavior , an integrative analysis of research finding remains that scarcity principle in consumer behavior, it refers that scarcity to the condition of resources shortages, it can affect consumer behavior. So, consumer behavior and resource shortage, they seem have close cause and effect relationship between them. For buying behavior example, when one male consumer with high shopping motivations, when he knows a scarcity arrtibute and thus are a vary limited resources, e.g. he allows to buy the product within 5 minutes , when the shop will close soon and thus a very shop time clising time limited. It can persuade the male customer to make purchase decisin immediately. So, it seems that intangible resource , such as shop closing limited time, scarcity may also be a fundamental phenomenon that influences consumer behavior, when the consumer feels that shop will close, it does not allow himw to continue to stay long time in the shop. The shop closing time nay persuade the customer to buy the product immediately.

It explains that why the influence of quantity scarcity and time restriction on consumer, this implies that when consumers' cognitive resources are not restricted by external environmental factor influence, such as shop soon closing time or web traffic to media, when the online buyer , he dislikes to spend long time to click on any website stores to choose themselves brands of the kind of product choice to make purchase decision. The online buyer may only click one website store to make purchase decision immediately.

So, it explains why online sellers can sell their products firm online stores easily, because their website stores web traffic is not busy at the moment. There are not many online buyers click themselves webiste stores at the moment. So, when there are many online buyers can click themselves webstores to choose any kinds of products in shor ttime rapidly. Then, their online sale chance may be influenced by " not busy website stores web traffic jam to media time factor".

Hence, it seems that when one consumer feels resource shortage, it may persuade the consumer to choose to buy the kind of product immediately. I suggest that people may not only differ in terms of how they choose to consume, this could include encouraging consumers , such as impact pf resource scarcity on price-quality judgement. It means that the predictable " panic shopping" in response, experiencing resource scarcity can also increase a sense of community by encouraging consumer to share shopping experience. So, product uncertainity , which is able to motivate behaviors, such as urgency to buy.

This, scarcity , also is known as paucity, is an eonomics term used to refer to a gap between the buyer purchase desire and external environmental factor, for exmaple time and money are characteristically scarce resources, to urge consumers to make purchases or else they won't guarantee next day purchase the product.

Howveer, the cost of using a resource is called the opportunity cost, the value of the next scarcity in economics connotes not that something is nearly impossible to finf. In common, consumers must choose between correct consumption and future consumption, for example, the COVID 19 crisisi may bring positive urgent time to save product, e.g. medical mouth cover protection product, when many medical mouth cover protection product buyers believe the brand of covid 19 medical moth cover protection products supply is shortage, they believe they ought buy the brand of medical mouth cover protection product supply is shortage, they believe thay ought buy the brand of medical mouth cover protection products immediately.

Otherwise, they can not find this kind of covid 19 medical mouth cover protection products to buy later. So, the anticipation to the covid 19 crisis will help some brands of medical mouth cover protection proucts, they can be sold rapidly . So, panic buying may be encouraged when the covid19 mouth cover protection product buyers feel a common brand share covid 19 mouth cover protection products shortage resource through a collection action. Hence, even the brand of covid 19 medical mouth cover protection products prices are raised, the covid 19 mouth cover buyers still choose to buy the brand of covid 19 mouth cover protection products, because they believe that they can not buy the brand of covid 19 medical mouth protection cover products later, when this brand of covid 19 medical mouth cover manufacturers won't continue to manufacture this kind of covid 19 medical mouth cover products again.

So, it explains that crisis and product sale time limited intangible resources can influence consumers to make a lot purchase decision suddenly. On conclusion, resource scarcity is essentially about current brand for a resource exceeding available supply. Resource scarcity occurs when demand for a natural resource is greater than the available supply leading to a decline in the stock of available resources.

However, limited time may be one kind of intangible resource shortage to influence consumers to choose to make the purchase decision to avoid that they lose the final purchase chance. So, the intangible limited time psychological factor may help businessmen to sell their products in short time, when the consumers feel that they have no enough time to choose any kinds of product to buy or they believe that they can not buy the kind of product later. So, resource shortage may bring position impact to influence consumer behavior in behavioral economy view.

Do they have relationship between organizational resource economic behavior and social needs?

In organizational behavioral economy view, economic

systems that shape behaviors and constrain access to resource necessary to organizations and society both. People are influenced to organizations as employees, consumers. IN behavioral economy view, economics is the social science that examines how individuals, businesses and overall societies manage scarce resources. Because none resource exist in unlimited quantities, even internet technology resource , societies must establish priorities and decide how best to allocate resources in such a way that meets as many needs and wants as possible . So, organizational behavioral and economics to explain why employees sometimes make irrational business decisions , and why and how the organization employee individual behavior does not follow the predictions of economic models . Because any organizational employees are emotional and easily distracted brings , they make decisions that are not in their self interest when they are working in organization. Hence, how whether it is more or less any organizations use themselves resource. It may influence the social whether it has much or less resources to society. It can use which interact within the organization, Why have they interaction to influence resource supply between orgaizations and societies?

In sociology, a social organization is a pattern of relationship between and among individuals and social groups. Characteristics of social organization can include qualities, such as division of labour, communication system, leadership , structure of a organization. For hospital example, it is one social organization, whether how it uses its resource , it can inluence whether society has how much resources can use. Hospital is one social resource organization (division of labour), e.g. doctors, nurses teams, cleaner teams, patient customer enquire teams, counter service teams. They are a major influence on social behavior and is the link between human nature reaching to the hospital organizational and social environment. Hoe many actual patients number , social need in the year, if the year , there are not many patients need to feel to go to hospital , then it can influence the hospital feels resource excess, or it won't need to use more hospital resource to serve its patients in the year. S, social patients needs and hospital medicine supply needs, they have close relationship every year. It means that the hospital's medicine manufacture material won't need much, it the year has not many patients or patients number is decreasing. So, shopital organzation hoe to need its resource, it has close relationship to patients number in society (nature, demographic, economic, cultural and social behavior patterns and consciousness). So, it explains why the social organization is the best of all organized human society, such as hospital organization example, its patients number will influence medicine resource need.

Another example is bus public transport service social passengers number choice to catching bus transport tool, it can influence whether how buses use oil nature resources needs. If the year , there are less passengers to choose to catch buses, they choose to catch trams, trains, ferries in preference, then due to every bus reduces passengers numer, it does not often driven , following the fixed timetable. If the bus stations often have no many passengers are waiting buses, then many buses are often staying in bus stations. Consequently, bus oil fuel nature resources need must reduce. Thus, social bus passengers number may have indirect relationship to influence buses oil fuel natural resources needs every year. It means that bus oil fuel nature resource use amount is influened by social passengers public transport tool choice needs. It is one good example bus public transport service organization seems to be one social organization.

Ecommerce organization resource management strategy

Why does in this e-commerce organization situation, online webstore speed must be the most important factor to influence its sale success. Information technology internet speed, online webstore design, online transation convenience transaction feeling (tangibale and intangible both resource factors) may influence its future clients number ?

In behavioral economic view, any organizations must need to use resources to carry on any business or working activities. Resources may include: management time to managements, working time to employees, information technology etc. office computer to administration, factory equipment to plant workers, plant or warehouse land space to logistic delivery or goods shelves, electricity, gas , water to workplace , even, employees number. HR to any department tasks. So, it seems that before any organization can finish any activities, they must need enough resources supply in order to satisfy any activities need. If the organization overall itself , even overall society. I shall explain as below:

For ecommerce organizatin example, any online trading firms must need to own high speed internet information technology resource to supply to any one technologic staff store to pay visa to buy any product in the most short time rapidly. So, its online store website speeds must need to be very fast in order to avoid to delay any country clients to carry on online transaction. If the ecommerce business organization can not support efficient, high speed internet service to let any countries online buyers to satisfy its online webstore purchase service. Then, any countries' online buyers may choose another online store to replace to buy its similar product easily.

Hence, convenient webstore online purchase service much be very important to influence this online webstore organization. It seems that technologic online internet resource must be the most influential factor to influence this online websore organization clients number. If its online website store can not supply rapid online purchase speed to let any one country to buy its products from its webstores rapidly. Then, its clients number may be influenced to reduce. So, in this e-commerce organization situation, online webstore speed must be the most important factor to influence its sale success. Information technology internet speed, online webstore design, online transation convenience transaction feeling (tangibale and intangible both resource factors) may influence its future clients number . So, judging whether the kind of resource is the most important to influence the organization's success, it depends on whether it needs to use what kind of resource to carry on its daily activities.

In fact, one organizational change has relationship to whether its reponses can have enough supply as well as its behavior can be influenced by the resources variable , the scarcity of any kinds of resources are supplied to be used. So, I believe that whether any kinds of resources are scarcity in the organizational environment, how much they are used, these any kind of resources can bring relationship to influence how organizational perceptions, interpretations and responses.

How an ecommerce organization resource affects society?

Why has online webstore's information technology resource close relationship t influence online buyers number and social job chance?

Organizational impact to the effect on an organization has any reponses to influence how on society chance. However, organizations can also have a positive impact on the economic satisfaction of a town. More oe less jobs supply to the wociety, which can be influenced by whether the organization can have effort to buy how much resources to be used in order to carry on itself any business activities. Hence, it seems that if the organization, such as the above online website sale product organization, if it can have enough money to employ web design professional to help it to design attractive website stores to let attract online buyer purchase choice, as well as paid higher internet service fee to improve its fee to improve its online internet speed in order to let any countries online customers can still click its website rapidly, even in busy online click time. Many people click computer mouse to enter ecommerce website stores in the same time. Then, any one won't choose another websites stores to replace its online sale service easily. Even, if it can buy many advanced computers to let its staffs can use the best quality computers to follow any client's ourchase transaction in short time. When , they confirm that whether the client's visa card payment can accept and what product he has paid to buy from its webstore. Then, the staff can know where the accurate address of the country , the client's product can be delivered rapidly. It will avoid to delay any product delivery. So, if this online store seller can have enough internet information technology source to support its whole computer information department staffs to wrk efficiently. Then, it can increase more online transaction chance in success. Consequently, it can grow up its online sale business, it will create many new potisition, due to its computer information technology department must need to increase employees to help it to deal any countries online buyers online purchase service transactions and online product sale delivery service immediately in order to avoid online product delivery service to global online buyers. So, it can bring more job chance if this online webstore organization can have enough effort to buy high technological computer information products to let its online customer service staffs to use in order to improve online product delivery service store to let global many online buyers' attention . Consequently, it can apply online webstore purchase channel to apply website purchase channel to persuade many global online buyers online purchase choice to its webstore easily. So, it seems that this online webstore's information technology resource has close relationship t influence online buyers number and social job chance.

How do organizational resources affect organizational change?

IN general, resoults indicate that organizations possessing greater stocks of historically valuable resources were much less likely to engage in adaptive strategic change, but also that this resource-driven disinclination towards change tended to have a begin or even beneficial effect on performance . So, in general, if one organization lacks any one of these three important resources. It can influence this organization's performance to worse, they many include: human resource , financial resource, phycial resources and information resource. However, managers are responsible to acquiring and managing the resources to accomplish goals. If the organization can have enough resources to be used. It can bring positive impact to influence its overall organizational performance, even, when it has not any resource scarcity, it can avoid negative impacts on the society, such as increasing jobs chance. Hence, scarcity of capital, human and social resources to be provided to the organization, it will influence the organizational structure changes, even employee individual work attitude is influenced to change worse, when he/she can not have the best resources to be used in order to raise efficiency or improve performance more easily.

How to build organizatonal resource using right psychology

The psychology of management is the branch of psychology studying mental features of the person and its behavior in the course of planning, organization management and the control of joint activity. The human factor is considered as the central point in the psychology of management as its essence and a core. Hence , organizational psychology plays a very important rolw at the time or recruitment very important role at the time of recruitment taking disciplinary action or resolving disputes between employees. HR focus and expertise mainly lies in dealing with people . So , it makes sense that the study of the human mind, how to use organizational resources efficiently.

The organizational side of pschology is more focused on understanding how organizations affect individual behavior, organizational structures , social norms, management styles and role expectations are factors that can influence how people behave within organizations. In general, industrial organizational psychologists use psychological principles and research methods to solve problems in the workplace and improve the quality of life (e.g. avoiding often waste industrial resources in manufacturing process aims). They study workplace workplace productivity and management and employee working styles. They get a feel for the morale and personality of a company or organization, e.g. suggesting to use skills and knowledge relating to psychology how to reduce same productivity level, but the organizational resources can be reduced to use. It is one kind the most efficiency resources using method to any kind of organizations.

On conclusion, industrial and organizational psychologists will often use science to study human behavior organizations and the workplaces. Their aims to help organizations to reduce excess resource using in any manufacturing process in order to reduce cost. Employers who need to attempt to learn how employees use resources to do work activities, it can bring these advanaages : learning how to use neuroscience to attract the right talent, retain high performing employees, because any organizations' resources will be used in order to manufacture any products or work activites by any employees in any time.

Employees are the ones who get the job done. They know how the organization and especially ho w their specigif team works best. So any one employee may be the important factor to influence the amount of resource use, any organizational resource use amount, it has close relationship to any employee work behavior. Moreover, resources, that is , group-level resources associated with shared relationship that foster a quality exchange of information and interaction between individuals within the workplace , helping any one employee to learn more about on the job training, use employee training optios to ensure department leader optimizes the employees' motiviation and potential retention. Aim to give opinions to employees to know how to avoid resource using waste method to achieve cost saving aim to the organization.

Robots whether can help organizations to avoid resource waste

To judge whether robots can help any organizations to avoid resources waste behavior. We need to know whether robots can own recyle function. How do robots helpthe environment? Robots can help reduce waste that is implemented by effectively sorting materials that can be recycled and put to use again. They can even help sort waste materials quickly and move efficiently than humans reduce the input power amd cost unsociated with such processes. However, robots also may help business organizations with recycling, instead of natural environment . For example, tobots may help organization facility cut operate resource cost and allowed to take on a second load of recyclables to sort throgh.

How robotic technology help organizations reduce waste? Advanced software has made it easier to plan out routes that can efficiently guide waste collecting the waste and recycling materials that need to be collected. It also makes collection more fuel efficient and reduces energy usage to any offices, plants, warehouses, business organizations. It seems that robots can help organizations to bring recycling advantages. We should definitely keep on teaching robots to recycle our waste, e.g. clean robotics makes waste management smart with a robotic trash can that automatically separates used and not used materials in workplace environment.

How to use technology to help reduce waste? There is no financial incentive to reduce waste. One of a few manufacturers of AI (arificial intelligence) powered recycling robots. We can imagine a future where waste-collectig robots will move through air land, and water, cleaning our natural environment, workplace environment conveniently. For example, now robots are being put on duty to help solve the environment pollution, material waste, recycling challenges. AI assisted robotis technology that can work with humans in workplace organizational environment to have robots to do a better job at sorting garbage and reduce the building materials is wasted, sorting trash is a dirty and dangerous job, recycling robots may help human to do thin kind of sorting trash job, even further atomic bombs soon could be delivered over intercontinental distances aboard " pick a back" multi-stage rockets by robotis assistance. So, in our future, robotic can be applied on those avoiding resource waste job aspects, such as degradation and resource depletion , reduce , reuse, recycle and recover, have always been needed to avoid resource waste to future global business organizations. When, AI machine learning and robotics could help us , more efficiently organization, digital tools and new business models.

How green robots are helping with environmental sustainablity?

Robots can help reduce waste that is implemented by effciently sorting materials that can be recycled and put to use again. They can even help sort waste materials quickly and most efficiently than humans reducing the input power and cost associated with such processes.

How robots may help organizations to avoid resource waste?

Waste robotics autonomous recycling technology integrates advanced waste technology to avoid the costly deployment to any organizational users, e.g. the clean sea robot is an autonomous, electric floating aqua-droue that sweeps and collects plastic trash that has collected in coastal areas. It uses a has collected in coastal areas . It uses a combination of computer vision and remote sensing basd on 3D laser scanning technologies . So, clean sea robots can bring sea environmental protection advantages to global seas. Future global sea environment protection organization must need its clean sea tasks helping.

Instead of clean sea rubbish aspect, robots can also help organizations to do digital waste management tasks, digital technologies and their current use in waste management transparent, more economic and more resource-efficient processes, better souring of current important robotis digital waste manaement, technological trends, are robotics,the internet of things, cloud, digital rubbish robotic can help organizations to reduce digital rubbsh easily. then, any organizational digital system can do more efficient tasks daily. Hence, robotics can help e-commerce organizations to do digital resource waste management tasks in order to provide high efficient online purchase services to any countries online buyers in short time.

How robots are applied to reduce waste in hotel organizations?

Reducing waste in hotels in within reach with the help of digital technologies. How are robots used in hotels? Throughout the hotels, robots are deployed to provide information, front desk services, storeage services as well as check in and cleck out services , with technology including voice and facial recognition. An example, of artifical intelligence in the hospitality industry is the use of AI to deliver in-person customer service. The robot is able to provide tourist information to customers who interact with it. Most impressively, it is able to learn from human speech and adapt to individuals. waste management in hotels is important or it is getting increasingly difficult to dispose of waste. Therefore, hotel resource management robots can help hotels to decrease cost of waste disposal as the start with: Using refillable dispensers for soaps, shampoos and conditioners.

Could hotel service robots help the hospitality industry on resource management of robotized hotels, e.g. avoding food waste in hotel robotized hotels, example restaurants robotics technology can help chefs measure, manage and reduce food wase. Morevoer, a restuaurant robots do not get waste and can perform to help chels measure, manage and reduce food waste easily. From a human resource management point of view, in that sense, robotisation may help automation and hotels to improve it service and reduce restaurant food waste cost.

How social change influences organizational resource management method

● What does management resource science mean ?

Although, management science could include the study of all activities of groups that means a management function, it generally include discovering, developing, defining and evaluating the goals of the organization and alternative policies that will lead towards the goals. So, management science is the broad interdisiplianary study of problem solving and decision making in human organizations with strong links to management economics, business , engineering , management consulting fields. Management science helps business to achieve golas using of organizational resources to produce goods and service. It is a contemporary approach to management that is an extension of scientific management that measures the worker to task mix and ratio to raise efficiency.

Thus, the nature of management science is a science because it contains a systematic body of knowledge in the form of general principles. Management principles are important in nature, but they can not be expected to give same results in every suitation. Therefore, management is a social science. If any organizations feel resources are shortages, they need to find that the main factors to influence their resources are often shortage. Management science may be one kind the best management research choice, because it uses various scientific research-based principles, strategies and analytical methods including mathematical modeling, statistics and numerical methods to improve an organization's ability to enact rational and accurate management decisions by arriving at optional or near oprimal solutions to complex decision.

● Why does management science help organizations to avoid/solve resource shortage?

Because management is a core function of every business and a number of theories try to explain how any why resource will be use rapidly and resource shortage causes to any organization. The core function of the management science approach is to compare possible outcomes. In addition, managers in various functions have aware of the potential contribution of analytical modes . So, the managerical science function involves arranging equipment perform functions, such as procurement, production etc. activities.

For drug manufacturing organization or hospital, clinic, medical service organizations exmaple, any kinds of drug must be important resource to provide patients to eat. If they have not enough drugs to be provided to the hospital, clinic, medical service organizational patients to eat. Then, their sicknesses may become serious suddenly. So, managing enough drugs stick is very important. However, management science may help any one these medical organization to implement rationality in strategic decisions: Choice which kinds of drugs purchase number, in order to keep enough drugs supply in drug store room. Understanding in a drug resource pool choice, due to cash available is limited to any one medical organizations.

Management science aims to avoid drug shortage to any one medical organizations. Such as this drug organization case, management science may help them to identify the processes, which kinds of drugs are needed to buy immediately, notice the areas of weaknesses, and realize the future possibilities and needs of the medical organization's patient customers needs. The approach makes the drug utilization of resources easier, since the framework can notice the availability of drug resources and the proper eat of them to be provided to any sickness kinds of patients to eat immediately when the medical organization can have enough drug stocks supply.

How to apply management science to help hospital better prepare for a drug shortage management method may include: Having a plan, the director of pharmacy should consider developing a plan for managing drug shortages, implement structured communications. Ask the right questions,instead of , hospital management also needs to know what is causing drug shortages. IN fact, drug shortages are caused by many factors, including: regulatory issues, and business decisions as well as many other disturbances within the supply chain.

Hence, in management science view point, hospital can attempt to apply mobile App technolgies tool to solve drug shortage problem, because mobile App technologies tool can be one kind of immediate communication tool, it can identify when the kind of drug will shortage and their impact on hospitals, e.g. how many the kind of sickness patient number and automates the entire life cycle of managing any kinds of drug shortage. Mobile App, communication technologic tool can provide clinical information that allows teams to understand and mitigate the ramifications for shorted medications. Any possible drug shortage solution in hoepital, it may be a management strategy that includes clear policies and producers for information. It defines a drug shortage is as a supply issue that affects how the drug store room's daily drug supplies.

Thus, management science may help any medical organizations to solve drug shortage crisis, it may help any organizations to attempt to reduce health care cost, one common solution for mitigating shortages is to keep more drug inventory, but drug inventory number can not be excess, in order to avoid drug out of patients (old drug) to let patients to eat in difficult. Hence, any medical organizations need to implement good pharmaceutical supply chain management strategy in order to solve drug resolve shortage challenge causes.

● How to apply management science technological tool to solve resource shortage to organization challenge?

Management science technological tool predict method may also be applied to water scarcity management aspect for government water supply organization, it may provide the scientific basis to apply optimum water resource management practices in the affected areas, methodological procedure for drought and water scarcity management or applying the economic scarcity potential method to rare earth elements highlights. It can capture resource is a useful approach as is it has an technological tool to avoid scarcity of resources to farm from atmospheric physic to robotic farm water resource shortage technological tool. A key component of this farm management approach is the use of information gathering concerns weather change. It aims to help farmers can predict when ther are enough rain supply to the farm land, they ought grow rice or fruit seed or vegetabe seed to farms. hence, it seems that management science method may be applied to help any organizations to solve natural resource or manufacture resource supply shortage challenge to any organizations.

ON conclusion, management science may be applied to resource shortage aspect, because management science is resource management technique. The two techniques are as follows: resource technique is a technique in which start and finish dates are adjusted based on resource constraints with the goal of balancing demand for resources against available supply. Any organizations may encounter resource shortage challenge. Resource scarcity is essentially about current demand for a resource exceeding available supply. Resource scarcity occurs when demand for a natural resource is greater than the available supply , leading to a decline in the stock of available resource . However, any organizational resource shortage may due to failure management, difficult management technique causes. The common types of resource management may include human resource management natural resource management, project resource management, financial management, infrastructure management , facility management enterprise asset management public asset management at organizational resource management aspects. Hence any organizations must need efficient and effective resource management strategy in order to avoid resource shortage causes.

In organizational studies, resource management is the efficient and one resource management technique choice is resource shortage solution leveling, to keep the enough stock of resources on hand, reducing both excess inventories and shortages. Any kind of resource management technique aims to ensure access to resoures and avoid supply shortages efficiency in their use, facilitate their proper and of life management, hence, effective resource management strategy may help the organization to avoid resource shortge challenge causes easily.

● Reasons to organizations need management resource strategies ?

Why ought organization implement resource managment strategies ? better utilization means a happier and healthier team helping to reduce being overburdened and stressed. Resources are used to their maximum potential, keeping projects on time and on budget. It helps project managers keep to reduce oversights. The reasons that organizations ought to prepare effective managment science to implement the most reasonable and the most efficient and the most effective resource management strategy, because effectively managing resources can help companies more consistently deliver projects and services on time.

This is because better resource management helps to improve insights into resource availability as well as improves timelines projections. Why it is importsant to have enough resources supply and resource management strategies implementation? Resources are important for the growth to one organization, even development for any country, for example, generate energy , one need fossil fuels, and for industrial with the development, we require mineral rsources . On macro-social development aspect, natural resources are getting scarce with the increasing populatin, so it is essential to conserve them.

Why do we need resource management to organizations ? Resource management is the process of pre-planning, scheduling, and allocating the kind of resources to maximize efficiency. A resource is anything that is needed to eecute a task or project, this can be the skill set of employees or the adoption of software. Due to large organizations might be dealing with multiple projects. Effective allocation of resources help project maangers to avoid to use resources inefficiently, e.g. human resources, financial resource, physical resource and information resources. Hence, effective resource management science strategy can benefit the organization team and overall organization.

● How applying right science resource management principle to organizations

Scientific management is an attitude and a philosophy to be accepted and applied of the method of scientific investigation for the solution of the problems of industrial management . They may include experimentati, collection of data, analysis of data and formaulation of certain principles on the basic of such analysis. It aims to seek the most efficiency for plant operations. The main objective is improving economic efficiency, especially labour productivity.

However, scientific management can be summarized in four main principles to determine and standardize the one best way of doing a job . A clear division of tasks and responsibilities. High pay for high performing employee, for Toyalor's scientifi managmement principle example, he proposed that by optimizing and simplifying jobs, productivity would increase.

Nowadays, most organizations in the industry make use of scientific management, e.g. hospitals, car and computer , restaurants, among others. The advantages may include : reduction in the cost of production, better quality products, benefits of division of labour , avoidance of disputes between labour and management increased wage, gains to owners/investors.

The main aim of scientific management is to develop all men to their greatest efficiency . The specific objectives aim to enhance production and productivity, decrease cost of production and maximize prosperity both for employer and employees having common interests (not opposite to each other).

● How Amazon e-commerce applies resource management principle to bring avoiding resource waste benefit?

For Amazon e-commerce example, it does not apply scientific management principle, due to it is not one product manaufacturing industry, it is online sale service and foreign delivery service organization. It ignores one of the key of scientific management, its creators genuinely believed that you had to pay higher wages to anyone asked to puch themselves to their physical limits. Under scientific management wages are paid to the workers as per the piece-wage system. Minimum wage is not assured, so every work needs to pay incentive wafe when he can manufacture more piece product, but Amazon believes that pay higher wages to any one can bring incentive productivity , such as it only provide online sale and foreign deli ery service to any one online buyer client, e.g. it can pay higher wage to the warehouse workers, because they need to cooperate with robotics to work hard and the human warehouse workers need to learn how to dominate any one warehouse logistic robotics to know hoe to delive and put goods to the right shelves in order to avoid to put wrong goods to the not right shelves position in warehouse.

So, in Amazon scientific management skill to workers view, its warehouse workers are smart workers, they need to know how to dominate any one warehouse robotics to do the right goods delivery to put on right shelves tasks daily. Their wages ought need to pay higher in order to avoid theig goods wrong delivery to wrong sheleves in careless. SO, Amazon feels that it needs to pay higher salary to the warehouse workers because they need have more smart and robotic control skills. When they and robotic to works together in Amazon warehouses.

So, such as Amazon warehouse workers case, Amazon ecommerce organization can apply scientific management principle to reduce resource waste. I shall explain as below: Amazon 's warehouses have save diffeent kinds of products to prepare to deliver to different countries buyers, after Amazon had confirmed that it has receive visa card payment from online channel by each online buyer successfully. So, it must have smart warehous workers, they know how to control and dominate any one warehouse robotics to cooperate to send every right shelf position message to every one warehouse robotis to know, when the warehouse robotic receives the right product delivery to the right shelf message from the warehouse warehouse, it will delvier the product to the shelf position carefully. So, avoiding none of any wrong goods putting on the wrong shelves positions occurs easily. When, every one, there has none any wrong goods are putted on wrong sheleves positions occurrence, the spending investigation time to any wrong goods putting on wrong shelves position, it does not need to any one warehouse manager to do every day, So, Amazon does not need to waste time to do any goods putting on wrong warehouse workers number, when it applies many warehouse robotics to assist them to work in order to raise goods delivery efficiency in warehouse, e.g. Amazon warehouse can apply three logistic robotics and one human warehouse worker number to do one goods shelf delivery task. Before, it needs to employ ten human warehouse, logistic workers to reponsible to do one goods shelf delivery task. I assume that the goods shelf can put total 300 pieces of different kinds of products per day. So, Amazon can reduce none warehouse logistic workers number when it increases three logistic robotics to help them to do these 300 goods delivery task per day. Hence, its wage expenditure must decrease. Moreover, logistic robotics do not feel tried , bored, overtime work, these three robotics only follow any one of warehouse worker's message to let them to know whether which kind of product is needed to put on which number of the shelf positiion. Then, these three logistic workers can remember where the product is putted on the shelf position and help any one logisitic worker to get the right product to already deliver to the foreign buyer's home from Amazon's warehouses easily, they must raise efficiency more than only workers , they work in Amazon warehouses.

Hence, Amazon believes higher wage can enourage smart logistic workers can have good performance to dominate how every logistic robot , e.g. avoiding to send wrong message to let any one logistic robotic to put wrong product to the wrong shelf number position. SO, Amazon can apply warehouse scientific management method to avoid warehouse worker individual wrong message delviery to any one logistic robotic occurrence, when they can receive higher wage, and the three logistic robotics and one warehouse worker cooperation relationship is the most suitable workers cooperation number.

Amazon 's warehouse does not need more nine workers to often move in the crowd warehouse space environment to avoid worker accident and wrong goods putting on wrong shelves number position occurrences both. Hence, Amazon can apply scientific management method on warehouse avoiding resource waste aspect, when it decides to apply logistic robotics and workers cooperation in order to avoid wasting time to investigate whether which kinds of goods are put on where the wrong shelves number positions per day tasks occurrence in possible and it can bring delay to deliver goods to the online buyer's home. it is one good example of scientific management avoiding time waste method to Amazon warehouse organization.

Can Robotic Help Warehouses To Avoid Resource Waste On Behavioral Economic View

● Behavioral economy view whether robotic can help warehouse to avoid time and human resource waste

IN fact,robts are being used in different types manufacturing to create more efficiency with fewer resource. Robots also reduce errors, to leass waste is produced. Less waste is produced and the robots are able to final and separate the small parts more efficiently than human hands can. For example, on environment recycled aspect, robots can help reduce waste that is incinerated by efficiently sorting materials that can be recycled quickly and more efficiently than humans reducing the input poser and cost control with such processes. So, robots can bring positive affect the environment, because robots use less energy and produce less waste.

As a whole, there are multiple benefits to using robots to fight climate change,e.g. robots can prevent pollution and emissions through careful monitoring optimize the manaufacturing processes to reduce energy consumption. Moreover, robots can help with recycling, the use of robots allows facility operators some new flexibility. Most technologies used in recycling allow to sort materials. The sensing robots (sensoes) allow robots to receive information about a certain measurement of the environment , or internal components. This is essential to robots to perform their tasks, and act upon any changes in the environment to calculate the appropriate response.

● How Amazon warehouse applies logistic robots to help
it to waste resource waste

Hence, although robots can take our jobs, because they can help organizations to avoid resource waste, and it can bring negative effect to influence we lose jobs. ON behavorioral economic view, robots can help employers to reduce employees number, but it won't influence organizational overall performance to be worse or inefficiency, such as Amazon warehouse applies logistic robots to assist workers to deliver the right kind of goods to put on every correct shelf number position rapidly every day. Hence, one logistic robot can replace at least 10 store workers to do goods delivery tasks every day, e.g. one store worker needs to spend one minute to find the right kind of good to deliver to prepare to arrange to deliver it to fly to overseas client. Logistic robots only need 10 seconds to find the right kind of goods from the near 200 number shelves in Amazon warehouse as well as they are putting 300 different kinds of goods on these 200 shelves in Amazon warehouse every day.

Because each logistic robot has very good memory. Each logistic robot must remember any kinds of goods , their putting number position on which shelf, e.g. when the worker needs to find the model laptop product from 300 different kinds of products,in Amazon warehouse. They are putting on 200 number shelves number following positions. IN general, human worker will need to spend about one minute to find the model of laptop product from these 200 number shelves in warehouse. For example, when one worker needs to find the brand Apple of one laptop product model: PHZ0123, when the warehouse has total 300 diferent kinds of products are putting on total 200 numbers of different shelves positions. Any one Amazon store worker must need to type this Apple brand laptop" Apple" name and its model number" PHZ0123 on the store computer as well as to search its putting on shelf number position from computer. Then, the Amazon store computer will find this laptop product to find its present putting on the correct shelf number position , e.g. 50 number of the shelf positon, or none stock record of all this model PHZ20123 laptop is sold out. So, Amazon store computer must need time to help this store worker to search this laptop product's putting on shelf number position as well as the worker needs time to walk to the right shelf number position to find this laptop product.

However, logistic robotic does not need to spend time to type this laptop product brand name and model number in order to search where it is putted on the shelf number position. The Amazon store worker only needs to speak this laptop product brand name, e.g. Apple and the kind of product, e.g.laptop and model number, e.g. PHZ0123 and its piece number, e.g. one piece number. Then, the Amazon logistic robot can follow the store worker's sound to find its past this kind of product's shelf number position memory to move to this shelf correct number position and finds it to deliver to the worker immediately. So, if the worker speaks 10 kinds f different products one time, then the logistic robotic can help this worker to find these 10 of different kinds products from their correct shelves numbers rapidly. Hence, it seems that logistic robots can help Amazon store workers to reduce each product search time as well as logistic robots can help workers to do goods delviery tasks. So, in logistic robotic behevioral economic vire, logistic robotics can replace many workers to do product position research and delivery tasks, store workers only need to speak the kind of product name, model, brand name and delivery piece number to let the logistic robotic to know. Then, the logistic robotic can follow the store worke's sending message to find the product's past memmory in order to tell the store worker, whether the product has how many stocks on shelf, or none of stock on shelf and where is putted on . Hence, any one store worker does not need to spend much time to search where any kinds of products shelves number position are. They only need logistic robotics to help them to do any kinds of products deliver to , or 20 or more different kinds between products location and the store worker's location. It means that the store worker only needs to stay on the same location to wait the logistic robotic brings his products comes back after he speaks to let the logistic rotic to know whether which kinds of products and piece number he needs . Then, he checks the logistic robotic's all products where they are correct or not. He may put all of these different kinds of gatherng products to the lorry to prepare to send to airport to fly to another country to deliver to the overseas client's home immediately when he confirms that all goods are his correct.

Hence, such as Amazon warehouse case, logistic robotics can help it to reduce many products searching time tasks and avoiding delivering wrong product to any overseas client's home rick occurence. Also, logistic robotics can reduce store workers number, because logistic robotics can replace 10 to 20 human store workers number absolutely. Otherwise, human store workers may have errors in their product search process, e.g. finding the wrong product from shelf or putting the product to the wrong shelf number position, but logistic robotics can reduce to 0 error to put wrong product on the shelf number position or spends long time to search the kind of product from the shelf number position. So, in logistic robotic behavioral economic view, robotics can help businesses to avoid products putting on wrong shelves number position error risk, reduce store workers number, reduce product shelf number position search economic time.

Organizational intangible resource management strategy

● How to implement effective intangible resources management strategy to achieve performance improvement to Amazon e-commerce organization? Why does non intangible resources effective negligence management to Amazon organization, it will cause worse performance to Amazon e-commerce organization any one e-buyer?

One efficient organization must need have efficient and effective resources management strategy in order to provide enough resources for its organization overall different departments cooperation effectively and efficiently. How to implement effective resources management strategy to achieve performance improvement? Why does ersources shortage to organization, it will cause worse performance? I shall explain the reasons as below:

For Amazon e-commerce organization example, it is one global the most large goods transport delivery service moddleman role between global online customers and their product salespeople. Amazon owns its webstores, so global any one country buyer clicks to its different countries webstores , then he/she can choose any kinds of products to buy from Amazon any one country webstore. However, the product is owned the another seller. So, any products are not owned by from Amazon any one country webstores. However, the product is owned by the another seller. SO, any products are not owned by Amazon. It only provides webstores to let global any one e-buyer to buy the product after he/she has paid visa payment. So, Amazon's role is one middleman. It needs to provide goods transport service to help the product's seller to deliver the product to whose e-buyer individual hoime in the most short time, e.g. when one China e-buyer clicks to Amazon China webstore , after he chooses any brands of computers product from Amazon China webstore, he makes purchase of the brand of comouter decision. Then, he needs to pay visa to Amazon 's China webstore . When Amazon confirms that ie can accept payment by the China e-buyer's visa. Then, Amazon will deliver the product to the China e-buyer's home within one week or longer time, the delivery days time depends on how much delivery fee, the China's e-buyer , he can pay. So, Amazon only can receive commision infomr from the computer brand product seller. Because Amazon can build famous loyalty of rapid goods delivery service provider barnad and its different countries websites can provide above one million different kinds of brand products to let global different conuntries eObuyers to choose in order to make the most fair and the most reasonable purchase price decision from its different Amazon different countries webstores per day. So, Amazon can help its different countries sellers to apply Amazon itself unique different countries' websotes design to attract global many different countries e-buyers to click to Amazon's webstores to find any kinds of products to choose to buy conveniently.

So, such as Amazon e-commerce organization case, if it hopes to attract global different countries e-buyers prefer to click to Amazon itself any one webstore more than other firms themselves webstores . Then, it must need have enough resources (tangible and intangible) both in order to provide raoid goods delviery service and many different kinds of goods choice provision service and reasonable price consumption channel to let any one countrye-buyer feels confidence and safe payment transaction and enough product advertisement, photo, price, function information in order to make final purchase decision from Amazon itself different country webstores more easily.

Hence, the tangible and intangible resources are needed to supuply to Amazon e-commerce organization. They may include: Product photos, price information, product advertisement which are shown to Amazon's different countries webstores , enough online customer service enquiry employees number, enough computers number, enough computers number, different countries offices and warehouses number, computers, internnet technology etc. tangible resource as well as customer service enquiries feedbacks, global rapid goods delivery transport service to any one country e-buyer's home, safe e-payment channel, providing to buy global any one country sellers their products in the most reasonable and the most fair purchase transaction. All ot these issues are any one e-buyer individual purchase feeling to Amazon. SO, they are intangibel (non-tangible) resources to Amazon. It means that if Amazon can let global any one e-buyer feels it's e-purchase service provision can let they feel more satisfactory , then they will choose to buy Amazon webstores any kinds of products more than other sellers their webstores products, because Amazon webstores can provide the kind of product of different brands choice, it aims to compare whether which brand's price is unreasonable too high or which brand's product's quality is worse, or design is not very atrraction. So, Amazon's intangibale resource, such as rapid goods delivery service, online or phone customer enquiry service, webstores' products information whether e-buyers can feel satisfactory, e.g. reasonable price, clear product photo many different kinds of brands product choice. All of these intangible resources to Amazon, they may also influence Amazon's future e-buyer number absolutely.

● How can Amazon raise intangible resource number to be effective?

SO, I explain that Amazon hadboth kinds of resources. They may include tangible and intangible resources. Internet speed, whether it is intangible resources. Internet speed, whether it is rapid or slow to satisfy global e-buyers online purchase speed and non online traffic jam accidents feeling. Amazon webstores any brands of products, photos, price information images whether they are clear to let any one global ebuyer to feel when they click to Amazon any one webstores. All of these internet technology resources to Amazon any one webstore will influence Amazon e-commerce organization's e-buyers number will increase or decrease . For example, if Amazon's China webstore can not let Chinese e-buyers to feel that it can not provide different kinds of brand products photos' clear image to let any one Chinese e-buyer to see the product photo clearly. When one Chinese e-buyer clicks to Amazon Chinese webstore to find any brands of laptop products to prepare to choose one to buy. But when he clicks to Amazon China webstore, he can not feel any one brand of laptop's photo is clear to let he feels. Then, theser unclear laptop photos may influence the Chinese e-buyer forgets his laptop purchase decision from Amazon 's China webstore easily. He may clcik to the another brand of laptop seller webstore to buy the brand of laptop from the laptop seller itself webstore. SO, Amazon's webstore design may be the important intangible resource to influence global any one e-buyer's visiting Amazon's any one webstore times or reducing to do to choose to visit Amazon's webstore behavior , due to they do not click to Amazon any one webstore websites again.

I recommend that Amazon ought consider how to design its any countries webstores in order to attract global e-buyers visiting Amazon itself webstores times number increase. So, global e-buyers' visiting Amazon different countries webstores times which will be Amazon's most important intangible resources to cause its future global e-buyers number. This kind of intangible resources may help Amazon e-commerce goods delivery service organization to raise its competitive effort,, because when one country's ebuyer feels Amazon can provide the most attraction and fair purchase channel from its different countries webstores. Then, the country's e-buyer will talk to his friends, families to prefer to choose Amazon if they have online purchase desire. Because Amazon's any one e-buyer , he .she will persduade his/her friends, families to choose Amazon's e-purchase channel., if he feels it can provide excellent e-purchase method to satisfy his online purchase need. Consequently, Amazon's e-buyers number may be influenced to increase.

ON conclusion, such as Amazon case, how to decide its whether which is the most important tangible and/or intangible resources in order to raise competition effort. It depends on whether how the seller sells its product, in order to concentrate on spending to increase the kind of resources number, such as Amazon e-commerce goods sale and delivery service organization case, internet webstores design intangible image dissatisfactory or satisfactory feeling which may be the most influential global e-buyers number increases or decreases. Moreover, Amazon's internet webstores design intangible satisfactory or dissatisfactory feeling resource may also influence e-buyer before or after e-purchase service requiry feedback feeling, safe visa card payment feeling, fair and reasonable brands of products price information and different brands of product photos image seeing satisfactory or dissatisfactory feeling , they are intangible resource asset to Amazon when global any one ebuyer must need to click to its any one webstore to find its any kinds of product to make purchase decision. So, any organizations must need to spend limit money to support its the most influential intangible resource , instead of tangible resources in order to increase clients number.

On conclusion, we can increase organizational resources on these several aspects: Organizational resources are all assets that are available to a firm for use during the production process or service process, such as Amazon ecommerce organization case. The four basic types of organization resources are human, monetary, raw materials may be tangible, but internet technology may be another intangible resource to today any organizations. Improving organizational resources aim to improve efficiency, it means as the ability to accomplish something with the least amout of wasted time, money and effort or performance as well as effectiveness, such as improving internet speed, and none online traffic jam accidents occurrence easily. It means as trhe degree to which something is successful in producing a desired result success. However, we can improve resources by these way, they may include : Review who manages resources within the organization, build an-up-to date knowledge raise and company wide resource pool, manage the resource pool in line with the market, focus on education and talent employees growth, keep the customers in mind, work on quality services or products, learn to use technology , such as Amazon needs to learn how to raise high speed internet service for its webstores, and avoid online traffic jam frequent occurrent to its any one country webstore.

To sum up effective resource management strategy can help any organizations to increase resource number. Resource management is acquiring , allocating and managing the reosurces, such as individuals, and their skills, finances, technology , material , machinery, and natural resources required for a project. Hence effective effective resource management strategy ensures that internal and external resources are used effectively on time and budget, resources may be obtained internally from the host organization or procured from external resources. SO, effective resource management can help organizations to save resources being wastes and finances being spend on the wrong things, a significant cost saving factor. Hence, such as Amazon e-commerce organization, it needs to know how to learn how to apply internet technology to improve its different countries webstores design, shorten goods transport delivery time, gathering more different brands of product prices, data and phoducts photos improving safe visa card transaction secret to increase e-buyer individual e-purchase confidence. When Amazon can concentrate on effective allocate limited resource to achiev ethese objectives. Then, its global e-buyer number may increase significantly.

V

How society influences organizational behavioral change

Human Behavioral network job brings social economic benefits

What does human network job mean ? Why may human network job be popular? Why human network job behavior may influence economy ?

Nowadays internet is popular to use. We can apply internet to find data , search any new things, even earn money. Why does internet

may become huma network job source. For example, e-publish may be one kind of new human network job. Any authors may apply internet channel to help them to sell electronic or paper books from e-publisher web store. They may apply facebook, you tub etc. any online

channel to promote themselves new books to let new readers to know whether when they may buy themselves favourable new topic books to read

from electronic publisher web store.

Thus, future electronic publisher industry may help any authors to build internet network platform to help them to sell and promote

ot advertise their any one new electronic or paper book topic to let global any one reader to choose to buy their any new topic books from electronic publisher web store easily and conveniently. However, it implies that electronic network platform author may be one kind of future new human network job in our societies.

How electronic network platform author job may bring economy benefit in macro economy view? A person can have few friends, contacts and still be very influential if these few

friends and contacts are themselves highly influential, e.g. one author must not need to know any one reader in global society. When they like to choose any electronic books from electronic internet network platform. They may become the author's any one topic book buyer, when they feel the author's any one topic book is fun and attract they make decision to buth the strange author whose the topic book from electronic book publisher's platform web store conventiently in short time. Although, they are strangers, they do not know themselves , but the reader can understand what it way that made Google from writing platofrm to create new creative mind and typing network job method to replace traditional hand writing book method for global authors. It will be one kind of new human network writing job.

Hence, global any one reader can apply an innovative search engine , such as google.com to find whether whom author personal new topic books are value to read from internet.

Then, the electroniuc publisher's web store may be new book store platform sale network to help the author to sell many electronic or paper books from electronic network platform

in short time. So, internet may be future new network plaform to help global any one author to create network writing job absolutely. Furthermore, internet may be popular social media

to help any one author to build goold relationship between his/her readers. It is one kind of new network, human network job. New authors do not need to buy many paper books to prepare to put in any one book shop warehouse. Their every book can print on demand to reduce out of book stock in any one book shop. They may choose to sell either electronic books or paper books both from any one book publisher web store. So, electronic network platform may be one kind of good writing channel to help human authors to create income and it can also help authors to bring new creative mind and new topic fun content books to let readers to know and buy to read from electronic publisher network platform.

Why does human behavior may be one kind of new human network job to bring global economic advantages. ALthough, it may be free income or without inocme, but the person does the network behavior, his/her behavior may be bring advantages to influence many other people's health. For this case, when a worker in a coffee shop in an airport gets a vaccination aganinst the flu, it does not only helps him or her stay healthy, but also helps the many travellers who might otherwise have been inflected if that workers caught the flu. So, the externality , the result implies the vaccination of even a part of a community conveys benefits to the whole community. For example, governments pay special attention to the vaccinations of school children, teachers, health mothers, and the elderly, categories of people particularly susceptible not only to catching, but also to transmitting a disease.

It is not accidental that governments are heavily involved with vaccination . When there are externalities, free market, fail to persuade individual incentives with society's

their the worker's decision of whether to get a vaccine ends up attracting whether other people get sick. The workers might not fully take all these other people's potential suffering into account when making her or his vaccination decision.

As Stanford University does many suggestions, understand this and tries to help them make the right decisions and so providers free flu vaccines for its staff and students.

Small pockets of unvaccinated individuals can allow a disease to gain a spread more widely well-being. For example, parent weighing the costs and benefits of a vaccine for their child is not always thinking of the consequences of that vaccination to other people. THese are markets in which subsidizing or regulating behavior can make everyone better off. Because the reason for requiring that a child be vaccinated before enrolling in school is not just to protect that child, because each child's vaccination affects others via potential contagions.

Robots take our jobs behavioral and economy influences
Robot job behavior brings economy influences

If one day robots can replace human to do simple, even complex jobs. They will bring what influences to our global societial economy.The popular economic refrain declares that the
global middle class is dying and robots will soon take our jobs, e.g. shopping center customer service jobs, library service jobs, cinema ticket sale jobs, restaurant kitchen cooker jobs,
even, bus drivers, taxi drivers etc. public transport driving jobs, accountant, doctors etc. professional jobs. Whether it is beautiful or petty matter if our future societies have many human jobs can be replaced to do from robots. Businessman must may reduce to employ employees and reduce to pay salary or wage, when robots can be replaced to do their employees tasks. But, societies must bring unemployement rate rises , due to societies will have many people loss jobs when their employers choose to buy robots to serve their clients or do any office tasks or customer service or cleaning etc. tasks.

In micro economy view, employers may save money in long term, but in macro economy view, it will cause unemployment ratio rises , even crime rate rises when there are many people lose
jobs in societies. These models of doom, though, fail to account for the hundreds of businesses riding the waves of change in their industries when robots may be invented to replace human to do many simple , even complex tasks in our future societies.

WE may image that one small factory needs to manufacture fishes canes to sell to supermarket, the small

, cheaper stuff and higher margin parts of the fishes manufacture industry. Before, this factory needs to employe many human factory workers need to help every fresh customer makeing the perfect fishing gear, designed for performance, durability, and cost in order to achieve to manufacture every fish cane in whole fished processing manufacturing stages. Every worker needs to spend about 15 to twenty minutes to finish every fish cane , till to delivery to any supermarket to sell. If this fish canes manufacturing factory can apply manufacturing robots to help them to finish any one working tasks , every robot can only spend five minutes to finish whole fresh fish cane manufacturing process. Thus, every robot can

help this factory save 10 to 15 minutes time to finsh every fish cane manufacturing process. IN fact, time is money, because when every robot can help this factory to reduce 10 to 15 minutes time to compare human worker. Then, this factory can finish about 20 fish canes in one hour if it can use robot to help it to manufacture fish canes. Otherwise, if this factory still use human workers to help it to manufacture fish canes, then it can finsh about 3 to 4 fish canes in one hour. SO, the manufacturing efficiency ensures that robots must help this fish manufacturing factory to raise fish canes number more than human workers. So, in robotic behavioral economy view, manufacturing robots must help this fish canes manufacturing factory to raise fish canes manufacturing number and deliver increasing number to supermarkets to prepare to sell every day. Robots can help this fish canes manufacturing factory bring manufacturing time saving, rising manufacturing efficiency, improving performance and reducing wages expenditure long time advantages in micro economy view. However, manufacturing robots can

also bring disadvanages to society, e.g. increasing unemployment ratio, increasing crime rate,
this factory workers will lose jobs and income, they need earn social welfare from government and increasing government finance pressure in short time, even long time in macro economic view.

Stanford University graduate program in economics, Scott lecturer explained that "in demand and supply economic theory for robots supply and demand case, robots supply number increasing may influence human workers demand number decrease. It sometimes calls " the efficient frontier".
No specific human beings were mentioned in any of economics classes. As robots supply and demand in market case, They (robots) may be purely theoretical " agents" who reached to the most reasonable sale prices in order to persuade any one businessman buyer to make manufacturing robot buying decision whether robots can help him / her to bring how much saving time , saving money, saving cost, improving performance, efficiency economic benefit before he/she plans to reduce workers number when he/she decides to apply robots to replace human workers in his/her factory or office or any service department, e.g. cinema ticket sale service, shopping center customer service, shopping center cleaning , supermarket customer service etc. service or sale tasks. When robots can replace human to do any one of these tasks in any organizations. So, robots may be human worker agents who reached to prices the way robots would react to a software command. There was nothing that explained why some people thrived and others did n't or why truly brilliant, hardworking people could fail when much lazier folks succeeded." Having been admitted to the Stanford

University graduate program in economics, Scott lecturer hoped to get his answers there.

How robots influence our future social changing? Using the right technology can be a boon to your business in this economy. For internet example, it is easier than ever to find well-matched customers all around the world, to stay in contact with them, and to more quickly design the products they want. If you focus solely on being cutting -edge, though you risk letting the technology

take over what should be very robust relationships with your customers , employees, and colleagues. IN nowaddays society, technoligical advances and cutomation, personal relationships in business are more crucial than ever. I mean that robots can not replace human to serve clients to let them to feel more comfortable and passion more easily. For shoe shop case example, if the shoe shop apply one robot to serve its clients to replace human shoe salesperson to serve its shoe customers. Robots ensure that they can not persuade every shoe potential buyer to make shoe buying decision more easily when robots need to contact every shoe potential buyer. The reason is simple, because robots can not touch any one shoe buyer individual emotion very easier.

If the shoe buyer needs the robots to help him/her to choose any right shoe styles when he/she can not feel himself / herself can make the most right shoe style choice decision. The robots can not replace human shoe salesperson to make shoe style choice judgement more easily. They must need longer time to analyze whether which shoe style may be the most suitable to the shoe buyer. Otherwise, human shoe salesperson may attempt to make the most right shoe style choice decision to help any one shoe buyer to chooce the most right style shoe because he/she owns shoe style sale experience, shoe style knowledge, the most important reason is that they can feel every shoe customer individual emotion to touch whether he/she will feel comfortable or happy when they attempt to help every shoe customer to seek the most right shoe style in every shoe customer whole shoe searching processing. Othwerwise, serving robots are only one machine, they can not touch or feel every shoe customer individual emotion whether he/she feel comfortable or unhappy or happy when they need to contact them in whole shoe searching processing. Hence, I believe that some tasks robots can

not repalce human staff to do very easily. Otherwise, robots may bring disadvanatges to let any one businessman to loss his/her customers, due to robots can not touch every customer

emotion to compare human staff in service tasks more easily. Robots serving customer behaviors may cause money lose and customers number lose to the shop in micro economic view.

Intellectual human economic behaviors
What does intellectual human economic behaviors mean ? I believe that when we choose or decide to do intellectual behaviors, then our societies will be influenced to bring economic growth in consequence.I shall attempt to indicate pollution case to explain how and why eithet our intellectual or foolish behaviors may bring economic growth or recession in consequence as below:
On one hand, for air pollution social case aspect example, if we only consider to buy cars to drive for working aimr or holiday leisure aim. Then, our societies air will be polluted. Our health will be influenced to bad. Our car driving behaviors may cause global environment air pollution serously. In long tiem, global air pollution will bring our

bodies health to be bad. Although, ourselves car driving behaviors may bring our driving travelling leisure enjoyment and comfortable feeling in short time, also we so not need to pay public transport fare often, but we need to compensate ourselves health economic intangible loss due to air pollution , when cars number increases, dirty air will cause ouselves health to become bad.

In the result, we will need to pay more medical expenditure when we are old age, due to ourselves bodies will become bad, due to we breathe global dirty air every day, due to ourselves cars pollute air in long time, e.g. 10 to 20 years, even 30 more without limited air pollution environment. So, driving cars behavior may be one kind of human foolish behavior and our foolish behavior may bring ourselves future long time medical expenditure absolutely.

One the other hand, water pollution social aspect, if we often keep much rubblish to pollute sea, oil exploration porcessing pollute ocean , ships gas pollute ocaen, then fishes will eat polluted food and drive dirty water, due to global ocean is polluted.

In fact, because human only to conside how to buy boats to carry on leisure enjoyment activities, or catch cruises to travel on the sea. Also, oil manufacturers only consider researching anywhere to find new oil exploration places to manufacture oil product, when their oil exploration processes pollute ocarn . Consequently, global fishes drink polluted warer or eat polluted food. They will have poison. SO, human will have high chance to eat poison polluted fishes, due to fishes are poison or are polluted.

So, human is doing foolish activities, we only hope to find oil exploration places to pollute ocean or we only spend money to buy ticket to catch ships to travel anywhere in global ocean. All of these human foolish behaviors will bring pollution to global ocean. On consequently, we will need to compensate to eat polluted or dirty or poision fishes, ourselves bodies health will be bad. In long time, we need have high chance to pay medical expenditure when we are old. So, pollution case may be one good example to explain how and why human foolish behavior may influence ourselves future need to compensate serious medical loss.

All of these human foolish behavior will bring pollution to global ocean. On consequently, we will need to compensate to eat polluted or dirty or poison fished , ourselves bodies health will be bad. In long time, we will have high chance to pay medical expenditure, when we are old. So, pollution case may be one good example to explain how and why human ourselves intellectual or foolish behaviors may influence future long time economic loss or economic growth or recession in micro and micro economic view.

On another water pollution aspect hand, if we often keep rubbish to sea, oil exploration processing pollutes ocean and ships' gas pollute ocean, then fishes will eat polluted food and drink dirty water, due to fishes will eat polluted food and drink dirty sea water because the global ocean is polluted seriously.

In fact, because human only consider how to buy boats to carry on any leisure water activities, or catches cruises to travel on the sea. Also, oil manufacturers only consider any where to find oil exploratin places to manufacture oil products from ocean, when their pol exploration processes can plooute ocean. Consequently, global fishes drink polluted water or eat direty food. They will have poison. So, human will have high chance to eat poison fishes.

Otherwise, such as pollutin case, it can infuence inflation or deflation. Consequently, the reason indicates supply and demand theory. If air pollution is serious, then we will consider health issue, global cars demand number may be influenced to reduce, when global cars number demand will reduce, global car prices and supply number will need to change to fall down in order to attract or persuade global car consumers choose to make car purchase decision.

Hence, global car manufacture number and car price will be influenced to reduce, due to global air pollution issue. Consequently, deflation will occur because when the country citizen usually does not spend much extra saving money to buy car expensive goods. Money value will be low. Otherwise, if global cair pollution is not serious, human considers to buy cars to enjoy driving leisure lives. So, global car demand is influenced to increase , also global car price will also influenced to increase.

Consequently, gobal human will choose to buy cars to drive. Due to we accept to spend extra saving to buy expensive car goods. Car sale price and supply may be influenced to rise up. Money value is influenced to reduce. Inflation may be influenced, due to global car consumers number increases, we would not have extra money to spend easily. Car expensive goods expenditure influences our spending habit to avoid to make car purchase decision more easily. So, human intellectual or foolish activities may bring inflation or deflation consequency in possible indirectly in macro economic view.

On conclusion, above pollution case explain that how and why human intellectual or foolish economic behaviors may bring inflation or deflation consequency as wll as economic growth or recession consequency as well as any goods demand and supply increasing or decreasing consequency. It implies that human behavior may have indirect relationship to influence any goods demand and supply number to either increase or decrease result as well as any goods price will be influenced to increase or decrease in micro and macro economic view.

The relationship between social change and human behavior

Why does economic changes may influence human individual behavioral change? I shall attempt to indicate shopping behavior and staying at home behavior to explain their case and effect relationsip as below:

Human behavior can be influenced by economic change or economic change can be influenced by human behavior? Why does recession may influence consumers reduce shopping desire? In social recession suitation, it is possible that many people lose jobs suddenly, due to businessmen lose many customers. They need to make decision to reduce employees number in order to continue to keep businesses. Consequently, many firms (organizations) their employees may lose jobs. When they have much time, due to lose jobs, they will feel to avoid to spend too much time and money to go to shopping often. Many losing jobs people, they will often stay at homes.

So, they will reduce time to go to shopping, then non essential products won't their preferable choice purchase products. Hence, recession will change many losing jobs people their shopping or consumption desires to avoid to buy non essential products often . Usually when economic boom, many people have jobs to do because consumers number must increase when many people have jobs to do. Then, many people can accept to spend money to buy non essential products often. Many people feel spend time to go to shopping can satisfy their purchase of any kinds of new products useful psychology or desire. So, recession is one good example to explain it can influence many people do not like often to leave homes to go to shopping easily. Many people like to stay at homes, becaue they feel worry about spending too much shopping time when they leave homes. Their staying home time is one good negative shopping behavior example. So, economic change may influence human individual behavior changes , they have direct cause and efect relationship in behavioral economic view.

May human behavior influence economic change? Is it possible that human behavior may bring the country social economic change in macro economic or micro behavioral economic view ? I shall indicate publishing industry example. Do you feel that if there are many students feel learning is very important when they read many books or many of students feel interesting to read or they have reading new books in habit, then it is possible that the country will have many students like to spend time to go to any book shops to choose the books, they feel that they can help they learn new knowledge. Then the country will increase students number, they often spend time to visit any one book shop every week. Their visiting book shops behavior which may become their habits. So, the country will increase students number, they often spend time to visit book shops. Also, it implies that visiting book shops behaviors may be their behavioral habits.

So, when the country has many students often spend time to visit book shops , their visiting book shops behaviors may help any one book shop to raise books sale chance. So, the country's student individual often visiting book shop behaviors, their habitual visiting book shops behaviors must may assist help any one book shop to increase books sale number absolutely.

Consequently, any one book shop , its books sale bumber must be influenced to increase to increase because the country will have many students like or feel need visit book shops habit in order to choose any suitable books to buy to read at home in order to raise themselves learning effort. When the country has many bok shops often have many students visit their book shops, then their books sale number may be influenced to increase. It explain why student individual visiting book shop behavior may help any one book shop sale number increases also.

How human productive behavior may influence economic development

May any country which citizen behavior assist themselves country development? It is one cause and effect economic question. I mean that if the country itself citicen can not concentrate mind or energy to choose to do one kind of industry in order to let themselves country can bring the most benefit, then whether the counry itself economy can bring the most serious economic benefit. I shall attempt to indicate these countries themselves indistry choice to explain whether these countries themselves citizen productive behavior may help themselves countries to achieve the largest economic benefits. I shall indicate as below:

New Zealand farmer individual wine productive behavior

For New Zealand country example, this country concerns itself effort is foucs on farming agricultural aspect. So, this country has many farmers concentrate on farming agricultural aspect. May New Zealanders choose to spend time to produce different kinds of wines, e.g. wine or red grape wine is for the people are eating meat, or they are eating dinner.

When these New Zealanders their behaviors choose to do farming or agriculture to grow and produce different kinds of taste of white or red grape wine drinking products job.

Themselves grape agriculture behavior will influence these New Zealanders themselves, they can learn how to improve different kinds of grape wine drinking products in order to achieve every kinds of white or read grape wines taste improving aim during their white or red grape producing process.

Why can New Zealander every individual white or read grape wine producers improve their white or read grape wine taste more easily? In behavioral economic view, it can explain that why any one New Zealander white or read grape wine producer can be encouraged or excited or persuaded to concentrate nervous and energy and effort to learn how to improve their white or red grape wine products easily.

In fact, New Zealand is one agricultural food export country. It has good natural environment resource , e.g. land, seed to provide any one farmer to produce themselves any kinds of agricultrual food products, e.g. fruit, or wine food products. Because New Zealanders know themselves country has enough natural resource . So, in common, many New Zealanders choose to attempt to do farming agricultural jobs in order to export themselves any kinds of fruit or meat or wine products to overseas or sell to domestic in order to earn profit.

So, when these New Zealand farmers number has been increasing every year. This country farmers will feel themsleves competition between this New Zealand farmers themselves are serious due to they may feel New Zealanders choose to do agriculture businesses in order to export themselves different kinds of farming food to overseas or sell to local to earn profit.

Hence, when many New Zealand farmers feel that farmers number has been increasing every year. They will feel themselves competition is serious. They must need to spend much time and nervous and effort to research what method is the best how to produce the best taste of white or red grape wine products in order to let local or overseas wine buyers to choose to buy his/her producing white or read grpae products to drink.

Hence, in competition psychological view, may influence many New Zealand white or reaad wine producers had been beginning to change their learning behavior on researching what method is the best in order to produce the best quality of taste red or white wine products to sell in order to attract overseas or local white or read grape wine drinkers to choose to buy his/her wine products. Their behavior will focus on learning how to raising or improving white or read grape wine taste method more than only focus on producing a large number white or red grape wine products. They believe wine quality is more important to compare wine producing number. So, New Zealand wine producers themselves wine producers behaviors have been changing on concentrating on researching wine quality method aspect more then wine producing number aspect in behavioral economic view.

America high technological productive behavior
For America example, US is one high technological country, it owns many high technological knowledge talent inventors, e.g. computer science inventors. Hence, US must attract many diferent countries owning high technological computer inventors choose to go to US to develop their computer science profession career. Also, it seems that when many computer science inventors or professions choose to go to US to develop themselves computer science new career. In behavioral economic view, due to their leaving themselves countries choice, which may bring

influence themselve country job behaviors need to be changed. They must need to adapt US new live. Because they will forgive their past computer science job. These computer science professionals need to spend time to adapt US new lives. They " past computer science job behaviors" will need to be changed to their new US any computer employer's new computer science job model.

Because their traditional computer science jobs needed to be forgot in their themselves countries. They will feel their old computer science job knowledge and behavior needed to change in order to let their US any one new of computer company employer feels satisfactory to accept their new working behavior in any one US computer organization.

So, on the other hand, many US computer company employer will feel that they must need time to accept any one new overseas computer science professions their working behaviors, their working attitude daily, because these foreign comouter science professional, their past computer working behaviors and working attitude must be different to US domestic computer science professions.

In behavioral economic view, these overseas computer science professions, their working behaviors and attitude must be needed to change in order to adapt any one US new computer company itself domestic or local computer science professional stafs themselves daily working behaviors and attitude because these overseas and local computer science professionals must need to team work together.

In behavioral economic view, it is only one way that foreign computer science professionals must need to change themselves past country traditiona daily working behaviors and attitude in order to cooperate with these US local computer science professionals in teams more easily.

Consequently, if these foreign compute science professionals can change their past working behaviors and attitude to let any one US local computer science professional feels to cooperate with them easily in short time. Then, the US computer company itself whole computer professional teams themselves efficiencies will be influenced to raised or improved by the changing past working attitude and working behaviors of these foreign computer science professionals. So, in behavioral economic view, only if US any one computer company hopes itself computer teams themselves efficiency can be raised or improved when it decides to employ foreign computer science professionals and US domestic computer science professionals. They need to work in teams together. They must need to let these foreign computer science professionals to know how to change their working behaviors and attitude to let their domestic computer science professionals feel easy to work together. Then, the US computer company itself whole team efficiency must be rasied or improved easily in short time.

● China share market investing behavior

For China share market example, economic development depends on financial market. Because if many Chinese have interest to invest to carry on shares buying and selling activities in orde to learn how to earn shares interest and share profit when the China shareholder can make decision to sell himself/herself shares in the the high price, then he/she can earn money when he/she can sell the China company's shares in the high sale share price position.

If China has many Chinese like to spend time to carry on investing shares activities. Themselves shares buying and selling behaviors will influence China has many companies can increase fund from many Chinese shareholders in order to have enough money to expand or develop themselves businesses in China in long term.

Consequently, when China can have many Chinese like to attempt to carry on buying and selling shares investing behaviors in China share market. Themselves buying and selling shares behaviors can help many Chinese companies have effort to increase enough money or capital in order to continue to do their businesses in long term absolutely. So, it explains why when many Chinese become shareholders , they can assist China will have many companies continue to develop their businesses if many Chinese like to carry on shares buying and selling investing behaviors in long time in China financial investment market nowadays in behavioral economic view.